UNBELIEVER TO OVERCOMER

Facing challenges to our faith with understanding and courage

MIKE DWIGHT

malcolm down

PUBLISHING

First published 2022 by Malcolm Down Publishing Ltd.
www.malcolmdown.co.uk

24 23 22 22 7 6 5 4 3 2 1

British Library Cataloguing in Publication Data
A catalogue record for this book is available from the British Library.

ISBN 978-1-915046-34-5

Cover design by Esther Kotecha
Art direction by Sarah Grace

Printed in the UK

Contents

Acknowledgements 5

Foreword 7

Introduction: Why the Topic of Overcoming? 9

Section One: First Things First

Chapter One: The First Glimpse of the Road Ahead 15

Chapter Two: From Unbeliever to Believer 18

Chapter Three: From Believer to Disciple: Part One 33

Chapter Four: From Believer to Disciple: Part Two 41

Section Two: Disciple to Overcomer

Chapter Five: Clearing the Way 54

Chapter Six: The Journey: A Ride or a Race? 66

Chapter Seven: If Life is a Journey, Does That Mean Salvation is a Journey Too? 74

Chapter Eight: Jesus' Call to Discipleship 81

Chapter Nine: Discipleship and the First Glimpse of Overcoming 91

Chapter Ten: Preparing the Way to Overcome – Hezekiah, Isaiah and Us! 96

Chapter Eleven: The Importance of Revelation 1-3 106

Chapter Twelve: Identifying our Enemies and Dealing with Fear 114

Chapter Thirteen: Facing Accusations and Temptations Head-on 122

Section Three: Crucial Knowledge and Understanding to Overcome

Chapter Fourteen: Assurance and Confidence in the Promises of God 135

Chapter Fifteen: The Death and Resurrection of Jesus Changed Everything 143

Chapter Sixteen: Adopted as Sons and Daughters in the Family of God 151

Chapter Seventeen: Persecution, Suffering and Death Are Not the End 162

Chapter Eighteen: Final Words 172

Acknowledgements

I must begin by thanking those, particularly in WEC and Betel International, who have inspired and encouraged me over so many years. Many have come through incredible challenges themselves and yet still remain on the cutting edge of life and ministry around the world today and particularly in the Far East. Encouragement may appear so ordinary but is in fact a precious jewel within the body of Christ.

I want to thank in particular Andrew Bowker for his insight, wisdom and godly example, steering me through the writing of this book. There have been times when I had little energy left to carry on and his gentle and persistent encouragement gave me fresh strength to finish the task.

Finally, I want to thank those who without knowing and at just the right time gave me a prophetic word or a personal word of encouragement after sharing on this topic of overcoming. It was the confirmation I needed in order to be faithful to the Lord.

Foreword

Mike has written a significant message for this generation. In the West we are often caught up with the 'glory' side of our relationship with God. When Mike writes about overcoming, he speaks to the oft-largely forgotten conflict and possible *suffering* of following Jesus. More than ever before, it is our duty and responsibility to prepare ourselves and others for the increasing challenge of discipleship in these days. Appropriate tools are required for this coming journey. Mike's book addresses this challenge head-on.

Mike is a missionary statesman and a trusted voice. He brings with him an enormous wealth of experience, acquired over forty-plus years of service in Asia. He exudes meekness and is just as much at home speaking to a large conference as he is chatting one-on-one with a newly arrived drug addict in rehab.

Mike skilfully builds up to a crescendo. He drives home foundational truths in the early chapters. He then traces the progression from the initial receiving of the gift of forgiveness and eternal life to that of costly discipleship which endures, perseveres and overcomes. Each stage is backed up by Scripture.

As you read it, you will be inspired not to just maintain your position but to press forward, to go into the hard places and to take back our broken cities. He teaches the reader not to focus on the storm going on around them in this post-truth world, but to tune into and obey that 'still small voice' (1 Kings 19:12, KJV) of the Spirit of truth. In a society that, in the last few years, has become unrecognisably dark, and where good has in many cases been repackaged as 'evil' and evil is repackaged as 'good', Mike gives us hope that our future is decidedly bright! We do not just hold the line, instead we advance, and we take ground – not as mere disciples but as the *overcomers* we are called to be, because we stand on the cusp of the greatest challenges and opportunities that the world has ever seen.

Lindsay McKenzie, co-founder of Betel International

Introduction
Why the Topic of Overcoming?

Writing a book on becoming an overcomer in Christ is an incredibly daunting and challenging task. I do so knowing very clearly that I write as one who has a long way to go in understanding the height and depth of this challenge, and whose experience, though many would consider it ample, still leaves me feeling apprehensive in approaching such a crucial and necessary topic.

My earlier books *Out of the Desert* and *Into the Land* (New Wine Press) were written after thirty-seven years of seeing churches planted in Thailand, and also overseeing church-planting challenges in nine countries of South East Asia. My original calling was to Thailand, which my wife, Wilma, and I still think of as 'home'. It was here that, together with our three children, Paul, Esther and Karen, we spent many privileged years getting to know and love the Thai people. Thailand continues to be a tough and challenging place to see the gospel transform lives, produce a multiplying church mentality and impact the nation. We were privileged to see churches planted and grow in both north-west Thailand (in urban centres and surrounding village locations) and also in Bangkok, among students and educated Thais.

As a reasonably successful missionary, at least in the eyes of my colleagues, it is so easy to fall into the trap of complacency and self-satisfaction. They both open the door, giving unconscious permission for the tempter to work like a termite. We have lived in areas where there are vast colonies of termites. So often we have been unaware of the destruction they are causing out of sight and under the surface. When the bulge in the timber is seen or the mud trail spotted, it is often too late to salvage the door, window frame, cabinet and even concrete structures.

Complacency and self-satisfaction do not seem the most destructive of conditions, but I suddenly became aware of their termite-like qualities, qualities that had the potential to do significant spiritual damage.

When Jesus was teaching on the work of the Holy Spirit in John 16:7 He said:

> But I tell you the truth: It is for your good that I am going away. Unless I go away, the Counsellor will not come to you; but if I go, I will send him to you.

At this time in Asia, working with WEC International and with an increasing heart and calling to WEC Betel worldwide ministry, I became aware of the Holy Spirit desiring to take me on a new journey. Betel's ministry is that of restoring broken lives of men and women out of drug and alcohol addiction and homelessness. I was actually in Ulanbataar, the capital of Mongolia, when this new journey became clearer.

I mentioned this journey in *Out of the Desert* and *Into the Land.* It was born out of the book of Exodus, the life of Moses and the Israelites, and particularly chapter 33. This involved a need for a fresh encounter with the Holy Spirit; a need to come to a new place of dependency upon God, taking off the ornaments of self-reliance; a need to come to that uncomfortable place of consecration where I let go of my personal ambitions and choose God's way, whatever the cost, inconvenience and outcome.

In these last few years, I have seen more clearly why the Holy Spirit needed to work more deeply in my personal life and ministry, especially as I continued to travel and minister in different parts of Asia. It is only in more recent days that I am beginning to understand some of the working of the Spirit in my life; hence the reason for writing this book.

What I am sharing in this book is dedicated:

Firstly, to the men and women of Betel International, many of whom have come through horrific addictions and found that the grace, love and mercy of God can break every bondage, bringing freedom, joy and a completely new life in Jesus.

Secondly, to those courageous believers in South East Asia who are facing enormous challenges to their faith today. They have taught me so much, and have been such an inspiration and godly example. Through their extreme hardship and persecution, they have shown a godly determination to turn even the darkest moments of life into opportunities to glorify Christ in these last days.

Thirdly, to the Church here in the UK where I now reside. The challenges we face today are probably greater now than ever. It is no longer popular to be a Christian. There is increasing pressure to compromise on biblical truth and blend into an acceptable and open-minded twenty-first-century society, where belief is fashioned and shaped not by the Word of God but the mind of people.

The topic of overcoming has never been more important than now. It is God's revelation and challenge to my heart, not just to be a better missionary, preacher, teacher and disciple, but over and above all of these important aspects of life and ministry, to be an overcomer by the grace of God, and be faithful to the very end.

Section One: First Things First

Chapter One
The First Glimpse of the Road Ahead

In November 2019 I was invited to be one of the speakers in Betel India, known as Asha Bhawan, meaning 'house of hope'. The story of the development and growth of Betel in India is brilliantly captured in *Don't Hold Back*,[1] written by Keith Bergmeier, who together with his wife, Lolita, pioneered this ministry in India, Nepal and Mongolia.

Their annual celebration conference is an inspiring time of thanksgiving, worship and dedication to greater levels of obedience and advance. Centres of hope and transformation have been established in more than twenty-three cities across India, and this has spilled over into Nepal and Mongolia. My small part in the amazing growth of this ministry has been in teaching discipleship to the up-and-coming leaders, and those in leadership positions of various levels across India, Nepal and also into Mongolia. The picture of seeing faces who have known the redeeming power of Jesus and his gospel now worshipping with freedom, joy and anticipation of the much more to come, has been and continues to be a moment of grace that is beyond price and description.

It was during this time that the Spirit spoke clearly and powerfully to me: 'Mike, are you content to prepare people simply to believe and achieve a reasonable level of discipleship, or will you have the courage to prepare, teach and live out by example the life of an overcomer?'

To be honest, after all these years of service I had dedicated myself to evangelism, discipleship and bringing a gathered community together. Woven into this would be leadership training and the key challenge to multiply life and ministry in others, so that they too could multiply

1. Independently published, 2019.

themselves in new communities of faith. But the thought of being an overcomer had not really registered with me at all. Everything was geared to ministry for the moment, with little or no thought to the future. Things were going to be different from now on.

I began to reflect on some of the early years of ministry and church planting. Going out to Thailand as a new missionary, the entire focus of those early years was to get the best Thai language I could possibly have, and understand and learn from the East/West cultural divide, with one supreme purpose in mind – to be able to love the Thai people as Jesus loves them, and then bring them to a place of believing that He is the way, the truth and the life.[2] As I reflected on this, some I knew had been faithful to the very end of their lives, but others had succumbed to the accusations and temptations of Satan, and the pull of the world had been too much to resist. Many others I honestly do not know how their spiritual lives finished. Had I really given them the truth of God's Word? Had I prepared them for the struggles, temptations and even persecution to come? How responsible had I really been?

Now in India among the recovering addicts, my heart was beginning to race once again. Looking around I saw wonderful men and women whose lives Jesus had miraculously rescued from the darkest of all worlds. This remarkable group of people had come from all parts of the country, north, south and east. They had been unmistakeably changed, not just by the kindness of people but supremely by the grace of God. As I pondered more on this, my focus changed to a question: 'But what about the future, the years and decades to come? Will I and they still believe, no matter what opposition, struggles and levels of spiritual warfare I and they may face? How much have I really helped and given them the armoury, strength and courage to 'stand and having done all to

2. See John 14:6.

stand' as Paul said to the Ephesian church?[3] Had I fallen into the trap of just assuming that once they had believed then all would automatically be well?'

I returned to the home of Ivan and Encarni Adan, the current leaders of Asha Bhawan. The following morning I began to write down some thoughts. I saw that overcoming is not a one-step achievement, but there are three distinct stages to be identified in Scripture. The first two stages prepare the way for the final stage, overcoming.

3. See Ephesians 6:13.

Chapter Two
From Unbeliever to Believer

I have been reflecting on my early days of searching for the truth and wondering if a personal relationship with God is possible. I had always gone to church with my parents, brothers and sister. Sunday was a church day. By the time I was a teenager my passion for sport, particularly football and cricket, dominated my week and weekends. My prime focus was to be a professional footballer, and nothing else was on my radar. Attending church with my family gradually became part of yesterday. My today and tomorrow now revolved around getting a trial for a top team and playing football. I progressed quite well, but to my great disappointment I didn't quite make the grade. My world fell apart. However, having a reasonably buoyant character I took the sideways move of playing football, cricket and now golf to quite a high amateur level. As I did this, I saw the need to pursue a profession and started training as a management accountant. I subsequently qualified, and to fit into my social cluster, bought a sports car. It seemed to me at the time I had now managed to tick pretty much all the boxes relating to enjoyment and fulfilment.

This was to change quite unexpectedly. One Christmas I was returning home from playing golf at Stoke Poges, Buckinghamshire, and decided on the spur of the moment to sing some carols at a church in Gold Hill Common, Gerrards Cross. Two things really impacted me. First, I had never seen so many people enjoying being together and worshipping; it was if they really were glad to be there, and not just fulfilling a religious duty. Second, their faces and voices sent a clear message as they sang; they believed what they were singing with all their heart. I soon found out that these people were from multiple backgrounds: doctors, nurses, accountants, solicitors, teachers, engineers, electricians, shopkeepers, to name a few. I wondered what had taken place in their lives.

My immediate response was to try to make myself a better person, and so for two evenings a week I volunteered to serve drinks and do odd jobs at Amersham Hospital. Unbeknown to me at the time, the Spirit of God had begun to work in my life. I first noticed this when I began to feel uncomfortable with my behaviour and lifestyle, whilst not many weeks earlier I was proud and comfortable with it. Weeks later I shared my experience of Christmas with the pastor of Gold Hill Baptist Church, who was to become a huge influence and inspiration in my life. The Christmas story and the necessity of the virgin birth of Jesus simply remind us and declare that salvation is entirely of God. He humbled Himself and became a man to do what I could never do, make myself right with God. Jesus did this by conquering sin, death and Satan himself.

The penny dropped. The Word of God helped me to understand that this movement from unbeliever to believer is not accomplished by a person's ingenuity, ability, self-awareness, determination or indeed my helping others or serving drinks to patients in a hospital. It was by the divine intervention of a loving God who sent his Son to be the Saviour of the world and be good news in my personal world. This lesson I have needed to learn and re-learn throughout my life. Even after more than forty years of serving in Asia, a tendency I have often seen in myself as I preach and teach is to think that by a clever, up-to-date approach and delivery of my message I can persuade people to renounce their Hindu and Buddhist upbringing, and repent and believe in Jesus. Whilst doing the best I can is commendable, if only I had emptied myself of me, hungered for a fresh new anointing of the Spirit, and clothed my sharing with a more compassionate and tender heart, I wonder just what could have been accomplished for the glory of God.

John in his Gospel makes things so clear that, whilst I can share truth, only God can cause eyes to see and hearts to respond and believe in that truth. Recovery of sight to the blind is the primary work of Jesus by the power of the Holy Spirit. That is what happened to me at that Christmas time so many years ago. Truth sets us free (John 8:32). It is only when the Spirit of God opens our eyes to acknowledge and believe in that truth that we can see and believe. And so this first stage of the journey requires the declaration of the truth of God's Word faithfully and passionately. But over and above that, the inner cry of the heart will always be, 'Let the rain of your Spirit water this seed and bring it to life from unbelief to belief, from death to life, from desperation to an eternal hope by the grace and mercy of God.'

The inner cry of the heart is illustrated in the Old Testament when the Israelites were in Egypt. They were literally slaves to Egypt, and there came a point when suddenly they knew they couldn't live like that any longer. Whilst there were some natural benefits of living in Egypt, the inner cry for freedom grew louder and louder in their heart.

> The Israelites groaned in their slavery and cried out, and their cry for help because of their slavery went up to God. God heard their groaning and he remembered his covenant with Abraham, with Isaac and with Jacob.
>
> (Exodus 2:23-24)

In the New Testament the opening of spiritual eyes to see is called revelation, and it is the work of the Holy Spirit. Paul in Romans mentions that this is possible because of the internal witness of God: *for God has made it 'plain to them'* (Romans 1:19). Even the most wicked have some internal knowledge of God. The conscience of unbelievers bears witness to God's existence; it is 'written on their hearts' (Romans 2:14-15).

Yali tribe of Papua New Guinea

There are many examples in mission of how the Holy Spirit has opened the spiritual eyes of men and women in extreme locations. The Yali people of Papua New Guinea is one such story.[4]

The Yali tribes were known to be fearful jungle warriors recognised in that area for their witchcraft and cannibalism. Their story is remarkable. It began in 1968 when two pioneer missionaries, Phil and Stan, arrived to share the gospel with the Yali and build a church. To most of us it would seem an impossible mission. However, today churches have been established among the Yali people. In August 2020 they received the Bible in their own language. The sheer joy on their faces as they received the Bibles is testimony to the power of the gospel and the life-changing ministry of the Holy Spirit. What a contrast to their previous lifestyle of violence and cannibalism.

The mission of Phil and Stan began in tragedy. Having heard that two foreign men had arrived to bring a new message to surrounding villages, they ambushed them, shooting 200 arrows into their bodies. Approximately three months after their death, another missionary family went in search of their fallen colleagues. Tragically, their aircraft crashed in the Seng Valley, killing the pilot and all on board except a nine-year-old boy, Paul. He miraculously escaped the burning plane and found himself in the same place where Stan and Phil had lost their lives.

Unbelievably, Paul was helped by a Yali man, who had not been in favour of murdering the missionaries. This man hid him, keeping him safe, until a later search party arrived.

Instead of a resurgent hatred towards the missionaries, they began

4. See *Premier Christianity*, September 2020 edition; also www.bibliatodo.com/En/christian-news/tribe-who-killed-missionaries-receives-christ-and-now-shares-the-gospel-with-passion/ (accessed 9.6.22).

to see Paul's survival as a sign. Against their culture and belief, they began to open up their hearts, and they invited other missionaries to move into their village at Holuwan. Five years later, thirty-five believers were baptised and a church was born. There are today more than 100 churches among the Yali tribes.

The families of Phil and Stan, through all the grief and pain, were comforted as they witnessed the transforming power of the gospel at work in this remote, hostile and seemingly unreachable tribe. All of this highlights the power of the gospel and the miracle of that inner witness that Paul speaks about in Romans 2 and the courage to obey the call of God.

When the light of truth shines, even among the most primitive of peoples such as the Yali, this sense of God is awakened. It is the same whoever and wherever we may be in the world. For my ex-drug addict friends, the inner witness was awakened by their sudden awareness of their desperation and plight. Many were on the very last breath of life. In contrast, many of my friends in Bangkok had all they needed. They were educated with a university degree, not short of anything, and yet in their plenty there was this nagging sense of emptiness.

For the Israelites living in slavery in Egypt, it was the abuse received from the Egyptians that provoked them to call out to God. We have heard this cry from the heart so frequently over the years: 'O God, if you are there, please will you reveal yourself to me, to us?' That inner sense of God was now being verbalised in a desperate cry for help. From the depth of their hearts, they knew this was not the life God had called them to live. From the depth of their hearts, the Spirit of God was beginning to shed the first rays of light and hope into their lives. From the depth of their hearts, they now cried out to God for help.

This is the first step towards journeying down a new road

What the Israelites did in Egypt has been mirrored down through the ages as the first step on this new journey. David in Psalm 34:6 wrote, 'This poor man called, and the LORD heard him; he saved him out of all his troubles.' Jeremiah at a tough time in his life recalled what God said: 'Call to me and I will answer you and tell you great and unsearchable things you do not know' (Jeremiah 33:3). Who can forget blind Bartimaeus in Mark 10:46-52? 'Jesus … have mercy on me' was his cry. The multi-talented Paul became aware too that he himself could not change, despite his religious upbringing and convictions: 'Who will rescue me from this body of death?' (Romans 7:24). Paul became aware that he himself could not change, no matter how hard he tried, even as a religious man, such was the power of sin. How, then? 'Thanks be to God – through Jesus Christ our Lord!' (Romans 7:25).

God is our Father, and he can distinguish a genuine cry from a cry to manipulate or a cry for attention. A sincere and genuine cry is a clear indication that the Spirit of God is powerfully at work. When we come to the end of our strength and resources, God steps in. The biggest obstacle at this point is often our human pride. The previous song of our hearts, echoed by Frank Sinatra, was that we did it our way; that now dissolves into nothing. It is a dark moment for the proud you and me, but on the spiritual side it is the dawn of a new day.

Two important things are taking place at this foundational moment.

1. The Spirit of God is bringing us to realise our absolute, desperate need of God

Our own darkness, storm and sense of bondage and hopelessness can be so different. Being a casualty in a world where unforgiveness, deceit and cruelty seem all too prominent has so many tragic components to it. But no matter how different your story may be to mine, one thing is common to all: God is bringing us to the same place to start a new journey. The testimonies of so many can be expressed in some of the following ways:

Hope in religious deities has proved fruitless. Disappointments and discouragement set in. Not far from where we lived in Bangkok, Thailand, there was plot of ground allocated as a legitimate dumping ground for idols, images once thought to be sacred and holy, that had now lost their influence and power.

> The idols of the nations are silver and gold, made by the hands of men. They have mouths, but cannot speak, eyes, but they cannot see; they have ears, but cannot hear, nor is there breath in their mouths. Those who make them will be like them, and so will all who trust in them.
>
> (Psalm 135:15-18)

It leaves an agonising cry: 'Is there no one who is unchanging, dependable, personal, and on my side, working for my complete good?'

The burden of self-reliance simply misleads you. Doing it our own way seems so right, and yet it is so wrong! We dismiss God's way, and we want to do things our way. Forget the easy way, the common way! Why is it that the ones who need God most resist him the most?

> There is a way that seems right to a man, but in the end it leads to death. (Proverbs 14:12)

The burden of discontent. Enclosed in a prison of want – bigger/nicer/ faster/ thinner – every desire brings a deeper level of discontent, the prison walls get taller and taller and acceptance seems to fade away into the distance. Who will love me unconditionally for who I am?

> Yet when I surveyed all that my hands had done and what I had toiled to achieve, everything was meaningless, a chasing after the wind; nothing was gained under the sun.
>
> (Ecclesiastes 2:11)

The burden of weariness has multiple strands. Chemical abuse may be more obvious, but other burdens and weariness stem from strained and broken relationships, insomnia, or striving for something that will never satisfy but only bring further stress and fatigue.

> Come to me, all you who are weary and burdened, and I will give you rest.
>
> (Matthew 11:28)

Is that truly possible?

The burden of worry, living under 'what ifs': What if I marry the wrong guy, or after dieting nothing changes? What if I fail and cannot do the job or please people? In the New Testament the Greek word *merimnao* is translated 'worry'. It literally means dividing the mind. Worry and anxiety split our mind causing high blood pressure, heart trouble, migraine and many disorders, and most particularly a wounded heart! Is there no escape?

> Cast all *your* anxiety on him because he cares for you.
>
> (1 Peter 5:7, my emphasis)

The burden of guilt. We try to dismiss the shame and sorrow, but guilt is like a consuming cancer of the heart. Psalm 32:1-6 tells us that the guilt of my sin can be forgiven, therefore pray to God while he 'may be found'. Can this burden of guilt be truly lifted and be replaced by peace?

The burden of loneliness is not the absence of faces but the absence of intimacy. The fear of facing death, disease and sickness alone, sadly experienced by so many in modern society. In facing the future alone, tomorrow's sky just looks so dark and foreboding.

> Though my father and mother forsake me, the LORD will receive me.
>
> (Psalm 27:10)

Does anyone care? Is anyone there to take hold of my hand and walk with me through all the tomorrows?

The burden of fear overwhelms and paralyses, and hope drains away into emptiness. Is it possible that the love of Jesus can dissolve all my fears?

> The LORD is my light and my salvation – whom shall I fear? The LORD is the stronghold of my life – of whom shall I be afraid?
>
> (Psalm 27:1)

We may all have experienced these in differing degrees. It is what life throws at us, but in this darkness there is hope. Darkness has no power over God's Spirit. *The light shines in the darkness, and the darkness could not put the light out.*[5] This is so wonderfully illustrated by the shepherds in the Christmas story. Their familiarity with darkness was suddenly transformed by the light of God's glory. This light is searching the depth of our hearts to reconnect us with God. The psalmist cries out 'he heard my ... cry' (Psalm 18:6), and he is waiting to hear yours and mine!

2. The Spirit of God is not only showing us hope, but also the starting point of our journey

The Israelites cried out to God to be saved from the Egyptians, and God called Moses to be the one who would lead the people out of bondage into the Promised Land. Throughout the Old Testament, God was preparing for his ultimate gift of hope and salvation, his Son Jesus Christ. He is the glory of Israel, and the hope and salvation of the Gentiles.

When we recognise that we are destitute and unable to change our lives, there is a challenge that Satan makes sure comes to all of us. What are some of his tactics?

He fills this world with religious options, anything that will distract us from finding the One who is the whole truth and nothing but the truth. There are an estimated 4,200 different religions in the world. Hinduism itself is a religion of 330 million gods. Sri Ramakrishna, a prominent Hindu saint once wrote, 'There can really be as many Hindu Gods as there are devotees to suit the moods, feelings, emotions & social background of the devotees.'[6] It's a confusing 'pick and mix' and random selection.

5. See John 1:5.
6.www.lotussculpture.com/hindu-gods-indian-gods-brahman-how-many.html (accessed 7.6.21).

From the beginning to the end of Scripture we are not given a choice of gods. In Joshua 24 he brings this final challenge to Israel: 'Throw away the gods your forefathers worshipped ... in Egypt, and serve the LORD... choose ... this day whom you will serve, whether the gods your forefathers served beyond the River, or the gods of the Amorites ... But as for me and my household, we will serve the LORD' (vv. 14-15). The battle is strong, confusion runs amok, and at this moment when our hearts are crying out for help the Spirit of God brings both clarity and a challenge.

One God! One way of salvation! One Saviour! One hope! From an all-powerful, sovereign God who is the Alpha and Omega of life, you would expect nothing other than clarity and simplicity. Jesus said in Matthew 18:3, 'unless you change and become like little children, you will never enter the kingdom of heaven.' It is uncomplicated, and yet pride is determined to keep us in the dark.

Satan is content for you and me to believe in Jesus the carpenter (just a human being), as long as we reject Jesus the Saviour of the world (human and divine). In Matthew 16:13-16, Jesus asks: 'Who do people say that the Son of Man is?' and the reply came: 'Some say John the Baptist; others say Elijah; and still others, Jeremiah or one of the prophets. Jesus asks, 'But who do you say I am?' Satan is content at this point, because there appears to be multiple choice, but no! Peter's eyes were opened to see who Jesus really is: 'You are the Christ, the Son of the living God.'

John's Gospel is a great help to us, and is so relevant. John shines light into the darkness, bringing unchanging truth, unshakeable hope and unspeakable joy. Personal encounters and miracles are woven through the Gospel, cementing this truth, hope and joy in lives like yours and mine. John's Gospel has a clear aim and brings us to the beginning of our journey.

> But these things are written that you may believe that Jesus is the Christ, the Son of God, and that by believing you may have life in his name.
>
> (John 20:31)

John's desire is that you and I may be so convinced of who Jesus is, that no matter what trials, persecution and hardships we may face, or how our future days develop, we will believe and go on believing, so that we travel to the end of life with unshakeable faith and trust.

This is the critical point for beginning our journey

The 'internal witness' of God and our ability to know him opens up a God-slot in our hearts to reach out to him for help. As we do this, the Holy Spirit begins his work to bring breakthrough and understanding of who Jesus is and his work of salvation for humankind.

> I the Lord search the heart and examine the mind …
>
> (Jeremiah 17:10)

Why? So that we might know him and trust in Jesus alone for forgiveness of sins and eternal life with God.

The final stage of starting this transformational journey with God requires us to answer a vital question. *If I am a slave to sin, hopeless, unable to change myself or cleanse myself, how can my life begin anew like being 'born again', and have reconciliation and fellowship with a holy God?*

Characteristics of a cry

We have said that crying out to God is an act of desperation and total concentration. It is a fervent expression of faith in God and trust in his goodness and power to act on our behalf. Crying out to God expresses the following traits.

Genuine humility

It is hard for all of us to admit that we cannot solve our problems or overcome all our obstacles. We need God's help. He delights in a broken and contrite heart that humbly seeks his aid: 'he does not ignore the cry of the afflicted' (Psalm 9:12); see also Psalm 10:17.

Unconditional surrender

When a situation becomes so desperate that only God can deliver you, a cry represents total and unconditional surrender. We don't try to bargain with God, but leave our lives in his hands. 'If I had cherished sin in my heart, the LORD would not have listened' (Psalm 66:18).

A plea for mercy

Apart from Christ, we have nothing in ourselves that merits God's favour. When driven to a point of despair or destruction, our unworthiness before God often becomes more apparent, and becomes the motivation for you and me to cry out to him for mercy. Because of the LORD's great love we are not consumed, for his compassions never fail. They are new every morning; great is your faithfulness' (Lamentations 3:22-23).

Personal helplessness

The temptation is to believe that we only need God's help with the really hard things! Remember, Jesus said, 'apart from me you can do nothing' (John 15:5).

Faith in God's power and resources

Our cry to God acknowledges God's ability to do what no one else can do. There is no plan B or back-up solution.

Special revelation

Revelation is the opening of the eyes of our heart.

The words of Scripture provide the knowledge and show us the way of salvation. James 1:18 clarifies this, saying that new birth comes through 'the word of truth'. We are born again through the 'imperishable ... living and enduring word of God' (1 Peter 1:23).

The Holy Spirit opens our hearts to the knowledge and truth of Jesus, enabling us to respond in faith so that we can receive new spiritual life.

> A new heart I will give you, and a new spirit I will put within you; and I will take out of your flesh the heart of stone and give you a heart of flesh. And I will put my spirit within you, and cause you to walk in my statutes and be careful to observe my ordinances.
>
> (Ezekiel 36:26-27, RSV)

This special revelation goes a step further, not only enabling us to acknowledge that Jesus is the Lord and Saviour of the world, but also that his life, death and resurrection enable you and me to be accepted, so that we are able to stand with the righteousness of Jesus Christ before an Almighty, all-powerful, holy and righteous God. Now, that is amazing news and amazing grace!

The gospel is *good news* heard, and then received through repentance and faith. God's gift of new life is received at this point. This is totally the work of God.

It is *good news* to know in your heart that all your good works can never make you right with God.

It is *good news* to know in your heart that your helplessness and bondage to sin is not beyond the help of Almighty God.

It is *good news* to know in your heart that when God created you it was also to redeem and rescue you.

It is *good news* to know that no sin or past traumas and failures in life have the power to stop you beginning a new journey with God.

This nugget of revelation brings unimaginable hope and joy. On the cross the sinless Jesus took on his body my sin and the sin of the world. Jesus died, was buried, and then rose from the dead, breaking the power of sin, death and hell. The way now becomes open for me to access the grace, mercy and love of God that will enable me to be considered by God himself a child of his kingdom and a member of his family. At this moment the Spirit of God gives a special gift: faith to believe and receive this gift of new life, eternal life. The door is open and I now repent, turning completely around to walk on a new journey with a new Master and Lord, and with a new power, the power of the Holy Spirit in me.

Angels rejoice. Heaven holds a party. Worship and praise to God echo through the heavens as I on bended knee enter on this new journey and new life with a grateful and thankful heart.

The obstacles that we have faced – the pride of life, my self-sufficiency and ability to help God out, the temptations to compromise and walk a middle path to please people – these will come back. Satan will not let us off the hook without a real battle. He will try to dissuade us from continuing on this journey.

Let us move on to the next stage of the journey with God.

Chapter Three
From Believer to Disciple: Part One

We have understood that God created us in his image[7] – to know him in a personal, intimate way. The climax of this relationship is seen in Revelation 19, the marriage of the Lamb. God's desire from the beginning has always been that his Son Jesus would have a bride: men and women from every tribe, nation, people and language to live in a new earth with resurrected, perfect bodies for eternity. What a prospect! However, we are not there yet. We need to look at the next phase of our journey with God from believer to disciple a little more carefully.

We have seen that the ability to know God is in every one of us. It is the Holy Spirit that opens up our eyes to see and our ears to hear and understand the truth of who Jesus is and our need of salvation. The sincere cry of our heart that declares the longing to be forgiven, healed, cleansed and right with God is heard. The truth of Psalm 40:1 is for us too: 'he turned to me and heard my cry.' Paul in Ephesians 2:1-9 makes this beginning stage of the journey with God so clear. The contrast is breathtaking – from dead in sin to being alive in Christ, from trying to earn our salvation by doing good deeds to receiving the undeserved grace of God. The entire work of Christ in coming to earth, dying for sinners, and being crowned with glory is by 'the grace of God' (Hebrews 2:9). Our redemption, God's act of buying us out from the slave market of sin, is solely due to 'God's grace' (Ephesians 1:7). The glorious truth that we are declared righteous through the work of Christ is a gift of his grace.[8]

To embrace and enjoy this truth and the reality of new life in Christ

7. See Genesis 1:27.
8. See Romans 3:24; Titus 3:7.

results in worship beginning to flow from our heart. And to experience this joy corporately with God's people can be a transformational moment. At this point there may be a temptation in you and me to say, 'I have now made it.' Complacency is the enemy of spiritual growth. The call upon our lives is to believe and keep on believing, which means directing the heart's attention to Jesus. Faith is a continuous gaze of the heart at God. Therefore, taste and keep on tasting the goodness of the Lord, pursue and keep on pursuing 'the glory of God in the face of Christ' (2 Corinthians 4:6).

So this phase of the journey is the beginning, not the end. Where do we go from here? What are the issues we need to face? What are the truths we need to hold on to with all our strength and with every ounce of determination?

My first awareness of this need

In my early missionary days in Thailand, I assumed that a believer was automatically a disciple, but in life and ministry I came to realise that this is not necessarily so. This stage is hotly contested by Satan himself, and no less by the Buddhist leaders and communities desperate to keep every Thai citizen as part of temple life and ritual. In rural communities the pull of the temple and the influence of the abbot was equivalent to being caught up in a rip tide. I walked through this struggle with many Thai brothers and sisters who, whilst knowing that Jesus alone could redeem their lives, still found temple life and Buddhism attractive. After all, right from day one in their lives they had been told that to be Thai is to be Buddhist. Therefore, would believing in Jesus make me a traitor to my own country?

Out of this situation so many questions started to surface, which I now realise reached out much wider than Buddhism, but in fact impacted every person from whatever nation and cultural background in South East Asia and beyond. Doesn't this transition from believer to disciple happen automatically? I came to the conclusion: No! Should a believer become a disciple? Yes! My New Testament makes that clear, especially Jesus' command in Matthew 28:18-20. It is to 'make disciples'.

If this is the case, then further questions immediately follow. What does this phase of our spiritual journey look like? What are some of the obstacles and challenges? What is the body of truth we need to receive, and for the Holy Spirit to imprint on our hearts? What are the decisions and life changes we need to make? What are the experiences that will enable the Word and the Spirit of God to make this transition in our lives?

This stage from believer to disciple reveals the need to balance two topics.

Eternal life and discipleship

Eternal life is a gift, but discipleship is costly. Eternal life is received through faith and repentance, but discipleship through commitment and obedience. Eternal life has nothing to do with works, relying totally on the completed work of Jesus, and discipleship is working out our salvation. Eternal life is guaranteed through justification, but discipleship requires life-long sanctification. Justification restores our broken relationship with God through Jesus' death on the cross, and sanctification is the process and work of the Word and the Spirit in our lives, bringing ongoing change and increasing godliness.

The motives and reasons for believing will be varied. For some, it may be the bondage, pain and disillusionment that has been part of their life for many years. For others, the weight of guilt and sin becomes unbearable. Often in a revival situation many have been confronted with the prospect of hell, hitherto never even contemplated. It now becomes a fearful reality. For the addict, the thirst for a better quality of life becomes unquenchable.

These and many more may be good reasons for anyone to turn to God. But there is so much more to a relationship with God than what has been called 'eternal fire insurance'. There is a greater journey and relationship that God is calling every single believer to, and that is discipleship. You can't separate faith from faithfulness; in both Greek and Hebrew it is the same word. How many times have we heard the comment, 'I am a man or woman of faith', but there is a disconnect between faith and faithfulness, belief and lifestyle?

A decision that brings no change to life or behaviour has little meaning. A one-time profession of faith with an optional obedience clause is not biblical truth, and cheapens the gospel. Phrases like 'accept Jesus into your life', 'ask Jesus into your heart', 'make a decision for Christ' are not biblically based, and unfortunately give the impression that you can accept Jesus and then carry on with your life as before. Jesus' gospel has always been a call to discipleship.

For Jesus, salvation was an offer of eternal life and forgiveness for repentant sinners, but at the same time it was a rebuke to the outwardly religious people whose lives were devoid of righteousness. The good news was anything but 'easy believism'.

Many have written about 'easy believism', and I have no intention of trying to overkill the point. But it may be helpful now to remind ourselves what this means. It can simply refer to someone who identifies with Christianity as opposed to Islam, Buddhism or any other religion, and because of this would call themselves a Christian.

A step up from this would be to believe in Jesus, pray the sinner's prayer, and claim eternal life, and then carry on as normal with life. The danger is that it can be no more than a soft, religious cushion to lean on, with no turning from sin, no repentance, no resulting lifestyle change, no commitment and no willingness to submit to the Lordship of Christ. These we will work through in the coming chapters.

In Thailand I have been confronted with what can be called 'nominal Buddhism'. This refers to a person claiming to be a Buddhist, but who never goes to the temple or listens to the monk expounding the teaching of the Buddha. When I first arrived in Thailand in the late 1970s, shop shelves were full of books on Buddha's teachings on enlightenment. Thirty years later there was a noticeable change; these books were few and far between, replaced by manuals on how to become a millionaire. However, whatever smugness I may have felt was short lived, as I soon became aware that Christianity is not immune from this 'nominal' tag or lifestyle either. A prayer recited, a church membership paper signed, or some spiritual moment experienced can all too quickly become a past experience and not a present reality.

Matthew in his Gospel is writing for believers about King Jesus and his kingdom. In chapters 5-7 he writes about the lifestyle of the kingdom. We are not saved *by* but *for* this lifestyle.

In Matthew 7:13-23 this is expressed in different ways. There is the broad way and the narrow way; you can't have one foot on both paths! A tree and fruit; each tree will be known by its fruit (also James 2:14-17). Again, the wise and foolish builders of Matthew 7:24-27; the difference is that a wise man puts Jesus' words 'into practice' and life.

Genuine assurance comes from seeing the continuing work of the Holy Spirit transforming one's life, not clinging to the memory of some religious experience or act from yesterday. This produces a genuine love for God and his people, together with a determined obedience to follow God's commands, whatever the consequences and cost. When this is displayed over a consistent period of time, it is evidence of the power of the Spirit of God at work.

This is the heart of discipleship. It is to consider every other issue in life as secondary to following Jesus. The implications of agreeing with this are huge, and puts us on a journey that Paul personally subscribed to: 'For to me, to live is Christ and to die is gain' (Philippians 1:21).

Key scriptures

> To this you were called, because Christ suffered for you, leaving you an example, that you should follow in his steps.
> (1 Peter 2:21)

> 'If you hold to my teaching, you are really my disciples. Then you will know the truth, and the truth will set you free.
> (John 8:31-32)

> Whoever claims to live in him must walk as Jesus did.
> (1 John 2:6)

When you analyse these verses, you see that discipleship is more than just believing, but lifestyle, how you and I personally live day by day. Discipleship is concerned with who and what shapes our lives. Is it biblical teaching and truth, or other outside influences? Discipleship is about influencing others, and makes us reassess what we are passing on to those we meet. Discipleship reflects Jesus and his Word, and not popular trends or opinion. Discipleship exposes my motive: how I live is either for me or for the glory of God.

The clearest way to understand this is to recognise that Jesus is Saviour and Lord. This is the major shift between being a believer and a disciple. It is the truth that inspires and equips us for the coming journey.

> if you confess with your mouth, *'Jesus is Lord,'* and believe in your heart that God raised him from the dead, you will be saved.
> (Romans 10:9, my emphasis)

The supreme work of the Spirit is seen in this verse:

> let all Israel be assured of this: God has made this Jesus, whom you crucified, *both Lord and Christ.*
> (Acts 2:36, my emphasis)

You do not *make* Jesus Lord, He *is* Lord! Lord means the God who rules… therefore bow to his Lordship.

A personal review of the key issues

The gospel of Jesus is a call to discipleship, not just making a decision. It is an offer of eternal life and forgiveness for repentant sinners, as we see in Matthew 7:13-23. It produces evidence of God's work in our lives, with the inevitable fruit of a transformed life, as we read in 1 John 3:10. Salvation is an ongoing process of being changed and 'conformed' into the image of Jesus (Romans 8:29). Grace, faith and discipleship lead to obedience, accepting that Jesus is the anointed Saviour and the Lord, the King of kings. Verbal acknowledgement is important, and this admission of the Lordship of Christ is seen in *doing* the will of the Father.

In Matthew 16:13 Jesus asked his disciples who people thought he was. Their opinions were many: John the Baptist, Elijah, 'Jeremiah or one of the prophets'. He then asked them personally, 'But what about you?' I wonder what your reply will be? To the disciple who has experienced the life-changing work of the Word and Spirit in their lives, they would agree with Peter: 'You are the Christ, the Son of the living God.' This declaration, revealed by the Father in heaven and by the Holy Spirit, is the springboard for continuing on the journey of faith.

Jesus is God: 'I and the Father are one' (John 10:30).

Jesus is Sovereign: he claimed equal authority with the Father (John 5:17-18; 8:19).

Jesus is Saviour: taking upon himself the limitations of human flesh. This sovereign Lord surrendered everything, even to the point of '[dying] on a cross', for us (Philippians 2:8)! 'While we were still sinners Christ died for us' (Romans 5:8).

Jesus is Lord: the book of Acts repeatedly calls Jesus 'Lord', whilst 'Saviour' is mentioned only twice (Acts 5:31; 13:23). Romans 10:12 declares that Jesus is 'Lord of all' – Jews, Gentiles, believers and non-believers.

Two important statements that take us on the journey.

- Grace does not grant us permission to live in the flesh; it supplies power to live in the Spirit.
- Faith like grace is not static. Saving faith is more than just understanding the facts; it is inseparable from repentance, surrender and supernatural eagerness to obey.

Chapter Four
From Believer to Disciple: Part Two

We lived in Bangkok, the capital of Thailand, for more than twenty years. During this time, it expanded and developed enormously. Underground and overground railway networks thread through the heart of Bangkok, helping commuters to avoid the horrendous road traffic congestion. Bangkok currently has four super-tall buildings; this refers to skyscrapers taller than 300m. The tallest building planned for the city is the Grand Rama 9 Tower,[9] When completed it will stand an impressive 615m high and become one of the top ten tallest buildings in the world.

The point is that the foundations for these massive buildings are crucial, and especially in Bangkok, which is built on water and soft soil. Extreme care needs to be taken with no shortcuts, especially as the capital of Thailand is at moderate risk from a distant earthquake, due to the ability of soft soil to amplify ground motion about three to four times.

Learning from this, I believe it is necessary to continue to lay the foundations with part two of 'believer to disciple' before we look at overcoming. Because, as we shall see later, in order to hold on, endure, and persevere to the end, as Jesus encouraged us in Matthew 24:13, the foundations of our faith need to be solid and sure. Paul is our example, laying a foundation with Jesus as the cornerstone, but he also gave us a timely warning to take great care how we build – see 1 Corinthians 3:10.

---

9. www.skyscrapercenter.com/building/grand-rama-9-tower/17620 (accessed 7.6.22)

True repentance and saving faith

Repentance is at the core of saving faith, and therefore discipleship, and they must come together. To repent means to think about things from God's point of view. Repentance is a heartfelt sorrow for sin, a renouncing of it, and a sincere commitment to forsake it and walk in obedience to Christ. It is therefore a radical change of heart, turning from self to Christ, and is more than simply saying, 'Lord, I repent.' Let's consider three aspects.

First, there is an understanding element, hearing the truth of God's Word, that sin and one's current life and lifestyle is not God's design.

> For the word of God is living and active. Sharper than any double-edged sword, it penetrates even to dividing soul and spirit, joints and marrow; it judges the thoughts and attitudes of the heart. [i.e. the totality of our being] Nothing in all creation is hidden from God's sight. Everything is uncovered and laid bare before the eyes of him to whom we must give account.
>
> (Hebrews 4:12-13)

Second, there is an emotional element too, in which our sin and its destructive working in our lives is hated. It brings out that inner cry, 'Enough is enough; I can't carry on like this any more.' Remember, Paul's response was not, 'Well, perhaps it isn't too bad, and my life just needs some minor tweaking here and there.' No! In Romans 7:24 from the depth of his heart he cried out, 'What a wretched man I am!' This was the work of truth (God's Word) and the ministry of conviction (the Holy Spirit) bringing him to the point of no return – it was to be Jesus or nothing.

Third, there is a personal decision to turn and renounce sin. It is a decision of the will to leave that life and lifestyle behind and to follow Christ in obedience. It is a decision that is shown by a complete change of direction; the outworking of this will bring challenges and change but also incredible joy in God's presence.

As our mind is gradually renewed, so we begin to understand and discern what the marks of a false and true disciple look like.

Marks of a false disciple

When faith is only an external response and not an internal, life-transforming reality and relationship with God, when money, riches and earthly success take priority over dedicating one's life to the primary goal of doing the will of God and serving his mission in this world, it is like wearing a spiritual mask or, as Jesus put it, being content to clean the outside of the cup and ignore the inside.[10] When the going gets tough, the false disciple pulls out.

Marks of a true disciple

Humility: God revives the spirit of the 'contrite and lowly' of heart (Isaiah 57:15). Revelation: God's truth cannot be discovered by human wisdom, as Jesus says in Matthew 11:27. Repentance: 'Come to me, all you who are weary and burdened, and I will give you rest' (Matthew 11:28). 'Heavy laden' (RSV) refers to the burdens we carry; weariness is exhaustion from the futility of trying to please God with good works; repentance is a complete turnaround.

Faith: those who believe. This is the flip side of repentance. Repentance is turning from sin; faith is turning to the Saviour. Submission: 'Take

10. See Matthew 23:25-26.

my yoke upon you and learn from me' (Matthew 11:29). The yoke is a symbol of submission and discipleship. 'Learn from me' means 'be obedient, listen and obey'.

Betel's mission is to bring long-term freedom and restoration to lives broken by drug and alcohol abuse. This is accomplished by building values, skills and character through living, working and worshipping together in a caring Christian community. Its centres are for men and women and are free of charge, operate no waiting lists, and are run by people that have experienced freedom from addiction themselves. The end goal is to help people not only escape addiction, but become productive, trustworthy men and women of character when they leave the community of Betel.

> Betel began in Spain in the inner city barrio of San Blas, Madrid [in early 1985] when a small group of WEC International missionaries began to care for the needs of a few drug addicts and marginalized people. Today its program and communities can be found in over 100 urban areas in 24 nations. While each Betel community has developed its own identity and personal approach in applying the Betel program to the needs of their people, Betel [International] embraces the same principles and shares a common ethos.[11]

The ministry of Betel in more than twenty-four countries of the world has been and continues to be a testament to the grace and mercy of God as seen in Jesus Christ. Addicts of all kinds – drug, alcohol or sex-related – have experienced the power of the saving love of Christ, and all three of these elements of repentance have been absolutely essential for the life transformation they have experienced.

11. www.betel.org/about-betel (accessed 23.6.22).

The privilege of travelling and teaching at Betel centres in India, Nepal and Mongolia will never leave me. On one of the trips I asked the question, 'What should Betel centres look like when there has been genuine repentance and faith towards God?' I found myself reading 1 Thessalonians 1, and the answer became clear.

Genuine repentance produces a God-given miracle, as seen in the life of the Church at Thessalonica. Work produced by faith, labour prompted by love, and endurance inspired by hope. Paul makes things amazingly clear. The gospel is not just words, but words accompanied by the power of the Holy Spirit. The Word and the Spirit together created life in Genesis 1, and now the Word made flesh, Jesus – who is truth incarnate – and the Holy Spirit create new life in the lives of hopeless people like the Thessalonians, like you and me.

There was deep conviction, a clear evidence of the work of the Spirit. They turned from idols and the works of darkness that had previously controlled their lives. They changed, and now began to imitate the life of Jesus, by the ministry of the Spirit. Suffering and hardship were met with overcoming joy given by the Spirit, because of who they now were in Christ, adopted into his eternal family. The truth of God's Word was welcomed; it found a home in their hearts. They followed their brothers and sisters in Ephesus[12] and destroyed the scrolls, books and teachings they had previously trusted in. Their changed lives were witnessed (seen, visible) by others, and they became a living example of the message they had heard and received. Their faith and faithfulness became known everywhere. It was not a one-off moment, but a continuing belief and demonstration of faith day after day. What a church! And what a thrill to be part of a community like this.

True saving faith is the outworking of true repentance from sin.

12. See Acts 19:19.

True grace 'teaches us to say 'No' to ungodliness and worldly passions, and to live self-controlled, upright and godly lives in this present age' (Titus 2:12). At this point we must also consider another aspect of true repentance and saving faith: baptism in water and in the Spirit.

Baptism in water

We have already mentioned Matthew 28:18-20 and Jesus' call to 'make disciples'. It is then followed by 'baptising them in the name of the Father and of the Son and of the Holy Spirit'. Jesus makes it unmistakeably clear that discipleship is linked to baptism.

Why?

For some, baptism is seen only as a physical and outward act, but is there more to it that caused Jesus to make this a specific command? As we read New Testament passages related to baptism, it becomes clearer. The physical act is a means of communicating spiritual and inward change. Being baptised in water is a vital link between the believer's death to their old life and their resurrection to a new life in Christ.

> … don't you know that all of us who were baptised into Christ Jesus were baptised into his death? We were therefore buried with him through baptism into death in order that, just as Christ was raised from the dead through the glory of the Father, we too may live a new life.
>
> (Romans 6:3-4)

For Paul it symbolised identification with Christ in his death, burial and resurrection, and total immersion is the only means that makes sense. The Greek word *baptizo* means to plunge, dip, or immerse, and total immersion in water makes this symbolism come alive. Going down into the water is a picture of going down into the grave (burial), and coming out a picture of being raised with Christ to walk in a new life.

Too often we have emphasised the human aspect and minimised the divine activity and the work of the Spirit in baptism. It is an act of obedience, but is also is a means of grace. In response to repentance and faith, the Holy Spirit demonstrates his power.

Kamphaengphet, Thailand

My wife and I had the privilege of church-planting in north-west Thailand, principally in the province of Kamphaengphet, best-known for bananas, especially the *kluai khai*, a small, round, sweet banana.

Marta Persson, a Swedish missionary, and Wilma (now my wife) had preached the gospel and seen several church groups come into being. Later I joined them, married Wilma, and we continued this ministry. Church groups emerged in different parts of the province, and the church in the main town, Kamphaengphet, grew numerically and spiritually.

The river Ping, a major tributary of the Chao Phraya River, runs through the town. Baptisms were always very special times of rejoicing and a declaration of faith in Jesus to the Buddhist community, to relatives and friends. One of the recent believers had a problem with smoking and just could not give it up, but desperately wanted to get baptised. After much discussion, I was relieved that the church leaders agreed for him to be baptised, although some were reluctant to do so. The Holy Spirit loves to turn faithful obedience into acts of power and life-changing moments. This dear man came out of the water rejoicing, his face beaming, and what's more he had no desire to smoke ever again!

That may appear trivial to some, but it was a pivotal moment in that man's life, and his testimony impacted many non-Christians, and encouraged the church in their path of discipleship. It leads on appropriately to receiving the Holy Spirit.

Receive the Holy Spirit

The Holy Spirit is not just a power; He is a person. He will never violate your will or mine, or force Himself upon someone. The Holy Spirit guides us 'into all truth' (John 16:13). The truth revealed so clearly up to this point is that salvation is entirely of God through repentance and faith in Jesus, the Lamb of God. Now revelation continues, and our eyes are opened once again to see our desperate need of the Holy Spirit to manifest the presence of God and demonstrate his life and power, and for us to become Jesus' disciples and witnesses. We identify ourselves with those early disciples of Jesus who, despite their best intentions, had denied Jesus. Now, having met with the risen and soon to be ascended Christ, they obey and wait for the gift of the Holy Spirit.[13] He comes to those who know the impossibility of being a disciple of Jesus with human strength and ability, and when we 'set our sails' to catch the wind of the Spirit, he does not disappoint. The promise in Acts 1:8 is supernaturally birthed into hungry lives of men and women whose one desire now is to glorify Christ here on earth and be his witnesses to the ends of the earth.

'Christ' means the anointed One, and Jesus identified himself with us and received the Spirit after his baptism.[14] The natural extension is that Christians too need to be anointed by the Holy Spirit. He gives life.[15] He gives power to witness, serve, preach, teach and testify, distributing spiritual gifts. He purifies, sanctifies and is continually cleaning up our lives. He guides and directs us in the path of righteousness and honouring God. He enables the presence of God to be manifest through us as our character is continually being changed. He unifies, giving us the grace and humility to live in harmony and forgiveness with one another.

---

13. See Acts 1.
14. See Luke 3:31-22.
15. See John 6:63.

Why do some believers never become disciples? I think it may be a combination of not understanding and not wanting to change. But when a person has this spiritual apostolic foundation, then they are in a position to be disciples transformed by the Word and the Spirit, new creatures in Christ, equipped and empowered to walk in the Spirit, and fulfil in obedience the calling and commission of God to the world.

Personal evaluation point

The crunch point… family, friends and the community around us.

What influence and pull do our family, close friends and the community around us have in the decision to be a disciple of Jesus? Luke 14:25-27 says this:

> Large crowds were travelling with Jesus, and turning to them he said: 'If anyone comes to me and does not hate his father and mother, his wife and children, his brothers and sisters – yes, even his own life – he cannot be my disciple.'

These verses have been widely misunderstood as hyperbole, a statement not meant to be taken literally. For most of us in the West, we do not live in an honour and shame culture like that of Jesus' day, but many of our Asian brothers and sisters still do today. In a culture governed by honour and shame, turning away from family business, traditions and culture to follow another tradition is akin to hating your family.

In this culture, there is no greater way to bring shame on your family. If a person tells their family that they are going to give up the family inheritance, business and revered traditions, the other family members would feel slighted, insulted, shamed and even hated. They might say, 'Why do you hate us so much to turn your back on all that your family, community and country stand for?'

We should never hate our family members or treat them in unloving ways, of course. Such behaviour has nothing to do with following Jesus. But when we follow Jesus, other family members are likely to misunderstand. They might even wrongly feel that we hate them. And while we are to always show our family members love, and invite them to follow Jesus along with us, if they force us to choose between Jesus and family, Jesus is saying that his disciples will choose him.

My friend Jamrat

Wilma and I and our three children, Paul, Esther and Karen were living in the town of Kamphaengphet in north-west Thailand. During the early years of evangelising, a village church was established in Thungmahachay, about a twenty-minute car ride outside of town. It was here that Wilma and I were married and enjoyed our special day with around 300 Thai believers from quite a wide area. Jamrat, a rice farmer, was the leader of this rural church. He became a very close friend to all our family, the children included. They loved to visit and play among the rice fields and banana groves, and sit on the small tractor known locally as the 'metal water buffalo'.

Harvest time was crucial for the smaller rice farmers like Jamrat. The rice farmers had an agreement to help each other out so that no one missed that small window of opportunity to gather in the rice harvest. Jamrat was the only Christian farmer, and they made sure that his turn fell on a Sunday morning. Despite knowing that his livelihood depended on the gathering of his harvest, Jamrat had no hesitation in saying it was not possible because Sunday was the Lord's Day. I remember him saying, 'How can I miss the meeting? Perhaps on this morning the Spirit of God will move powerfully among us. I can't afford to be working in the fields and to miss a time like this.'

Today in the West we might find it difficult to appreciate Jamrat's stand. We might not think twice about missing a few services to do something important like gathering in the harvest. The lesson I learned from Jamrat was that to follow Jesus is an incredible privilege, and any cost or sacrifice was minimal compared to all that Jesus did for him and for us on the cross.[16]

> And everyone who has left houses or brothers or sisters or father or mother or children or fields for my sake will receive a hundred times as much and will inherit eternal life.
>
> (Matthew 19:29)

This is not easy. It will feel like dying, which is exactly what Jesus says discipleship is like. The disciple is to take up their cross and follow him. The cross was an instrument of death, and here symbolises the necessity of total commitment even unto death.

Personal relationship of a disciple to Jesus

The beginning of the journey is receiving Jesus as Saviour and Lord. This new birth, spiritual growth and developing relationship with Jesus is dependent on an ongoing desire to learn from him, obey him, trust him, remain in him and to serve him.

Personal cost of discipleship summarised

Discipleship must be carefully considered. Complete surrender means that discipleship is not a seasonal or occasional pastime. It welcomes

16. Jamrat was a Thai village rice farmer who became the leader at the church we were married in. I took his funeral many years ago.

Jesus and his Lordship over our life as first priority, even before family and close friends. It may result in persecution and untimely death, but the promise of eternal life gives strength and courage to endure to the end.

As we finish this chapter and look at what an overcomer in Christ is, it may be helpful to reflect on a few important questions:

1. Would you consider yourself to be a believer or a disciple? Review your personal journey.
2. Is Jesus both Saviour and Lord? Identify some of your current struggles to accept the Lordship of Christ.
3. What has a negative pull against your desire to be a disciple? How can you move forward?
4. Complacency is the enemy of spiritual growth. What can make you complacent?

Section Two: Disciple to Overcomer

Chapter Five
Clearing the Way

I have tried to lay a basic understanding of the journey from unbeliever to disciple, so that no storm will be able to destroy or wash away the foundation of our faith and hope in the Lord Jesus. At each stage, including the one we are now starting on, it is necessary to ask three questions:

> What truths do I need to know and receive?
>
> What experience do I need to embrace and live by?
>
> What obstacles and challenges do I need to be aware of and overcome?

This last question about obstacles and challenges opens up this next phase: from disciple to overcomer. I am aware of the significant challenge of being an overcomer. It is firstly a personal road I am travelling on today, and I share from this perspective. However, like most preaching and teaching, it is double-sided – for myself first and also to help others too.

If ever there was a time to encourage and spur one another on, it is now. I was writing this during the Coronavirus pandemic; the second lockdown was extremely tough and life-threatening. Coming from this, my underlying motive as we move through the coming chapters is to encourage.

> But encourage one another daily, as long as it is called Today, so that none of you may be hardened by sin's deceitfulness.
>
> (Hebrews 3:13)

Finally, be strong in the Lord and in his mighty power.

(Ephesians 6:10)

Revelation encourages all of us to be or become overcomers. The Olympic Games were named after the city in Greece where they were held, Olympia. It is believed that they began around 776BC. Men competed for an olive wreath, which was basically a crown made of olive leaves. Paul would have been well aware of this athletic event and its strict training requirements. He was also aware that only one person could win the prize, and that it was received when the race was completed. In the next chapter we pick up on this and Paul's encouragement to us all to finish the race, and in that sense, we are all winners and receive the prize. Yes, we can all be overcomers, but the condition for being one is to continue in the faith until the end.

Paul is an inspiration to us both in personal encouragement and in equipping one another in the body of Christ. And if I have one desire it is to do just that. 'Be strong' is a command that runs through Scripture, and is often linked with 'do not be afraid', 'do not be dismayed', 'do not be troubled', 'do not fear', 'do not be anxious'. We need to hear the words 'be strong', especially when…

Facing a challenge or taking up responsibility that is above and beyond our natural ability. Whether we are discovering how to share our faith, restoring peace in a broken relationship, or thrust suddenly into a leadership role, we can identify with Joshua's experience after the death of Moses. The passing of Moses left him feeling inadequate to pick up the mantle of leading Israel. He needed to hear these words many times, and we are no different today.

Joshua 1:6: 'Be strong and courageous'. Verse 7: 'Be strong and very courageous.' Verse 9: 'Have I not commanded you? Be strong and courageous.' Verse 18: 'Only be strong and courageous!'

As Joshua placed one foot in front of the other and moved forward he was most likely feeling anything but strong and courageous, with the nagging thought, 'Surely not… we can't, can we!' In difficult challenges we discover how fragile our faith is, and yet Jesus reminds us in Matthew 17:20 that faith the size of a grain of mustard seed is enough. Jesus is speaking figuratively about the incalculable power of God when unleashed in the lives of those with true faith.

We need to hear the words 'be strong', especially when…

Facing opposition that appears overwhelming. We may be outnumbered and outgunned by non-Christian colleagues at work, at home among family members, or in a mission situation where we feel alone and isolated against organised opposition. Joshua experienced this as he approached Jericho with an ill-prepared and ill-equipped nation against an enemy that was equipped with all the state-of-the-art military equipment of the day.

Time and time again this scenario is played out in the Old Testament, and never more so than in the time of the prophet Haggai. Having completed the foundations of the Temple with great rejoicing,[17] this success was opposed. The Samaritans and other neighbours, who feared the implications of a rebuilt Temple, opposed it vigorously, and the work came to a halt. What now? God speaks through Haggai to Zerubbabel, the governor of Judah, and Joshua, the high priest.

17. See Ezra 3:8-10.

> 'But now be strong, O Zerubbabel,' declares the LORD. 'Be strong, O Joshua … Be strong, all you people of the land,' declares the LORD, 'and work. For I am with you,' declares the LORD Almighty.
>
> (Haggai 2:4)

In the New Testament, Paul urges the Ephesians never to retreat, no matter how great the opposition. The armour described in Ephesians 6:10-17 has no protection for the back, and only protects you standing your ground or moving forward.

Paul's life is a testimony to the truth of God's Word and the power of the Holy Spirit to abound in every good work, no matter how tough situations become. Whether opposition came from Demetrius in Ephesus or at the time that he wrote to Timothy[18] in the last months of his life through Alexander the metalworker, he was still encouraging and equipping, writing as a spiritual father to his son in Christ. His personal testimony spurs us on too, that through these times the Lord 'stood at [his] side and gave [him] strength' (2 Timothy 4:17).

> You then, my son, be strong in the grace that is in Christ Jesus.
>
> (2 Timothy 2:1)

Christmas and New Year 2020

It was at Christmas 2019 that the Lord confirmed my personal need to look at what becoming an overcomer really means. On the first Sunday in 2020 I was asked to preach at the church where I had been the pastor, and where I am now a member. There was only one topic to speak on!

18. See 2 Timothy 4:14.

The beginning of the New Year can be a struggle to balance fears and hopes. The tendency in many of us is either to be pessimistic or optimistic, and lodged in the middle is the nation's beloved New Year resolutions. Ambitious goals are often a feature of the New Year, and despite high failure rates, we keep doing it, year after year. Fitness-related resolutions, getting in shape, losing weight, and eating better has probably landed on top or near the top of the January to-do list, and is no doubt revisited several times during the year.

One of the downsides with resolutions is that in our mind we see them as to do with stopping something rather than accomplishing something, and we soon feel overwhelmed and discouraged. Motivation is the initiative to start a task, but it takes dedication, that internal desire backed by behaviour and action, to accomplish it.

The application of this to the spiritual life is not hard to see. Motivation may see us beginning the New Year well, but only dedication will enable us to finish well. Because our walk with God is not linear (i.e. the hoped-for, nice, smooth, gradual A, followed by B, C, etc.). Time and time again Scripture reminds us that there is an internal battle between the flesh and the spirit. The weakness in many of us is that we want God's best at the lowest price! Jesus tells us in John 10:10 that we have an enemy who is hell-bent to 'steal … kill and destroy'. Satan attempts to cause us to become offended with God, to end our fellowship with Him, to halt our development of Christian character, to prevent us from bearing more fruit, and finally come to the point of giving up on God.

My personal challenge entering 2020

I want to share at a personal level, trusting that what I say will resonate in your spirit too.

Spiritually, at New Year I start to dream, and although that is biblical, it can be unrealistic, and fall into the same category as resolutions. I long to return to Asia as much as possible. I dream of preaching to the unreached and seeing them respond to the gospel. I dream of teaching to the disadvantaged, to addicts, to the struggling churches and Christians in persecuted countries, and seeing the Holy Spirit work miracles in their lives as they respond to truth that will set them free. I dream of encouraging discouraged missionaries who have given up careers and home comforts and travelled to unreceptive nations, and have struggled to see any fruit in ministry.

I trust that some of this will become reality, but I am hearing a more important message that undergirds everything we have said to date.

I had that familiar tug in my spirit that I was not really listening to the Holy Spirit. 'Mike, as you enter into this New Year, I want you to focus not on what you will do, but what you will overcome.'

Motivation may enable you to start well, but only dedication will enable you to finish well. Something new, powerful, significant and life-changing needs to take place for this to happen. You may start this year in a reasonably good, spiritual place, but how will it finish?

Will my motivation become a casualty to temptation, trials and political pressure?

Will my faith and love grow cold?

Will the fear of suffering and persecution cause me to turn back?

Will the pressure to live according to the desires of modern society cause me to 'run with the hare and hunt with the hounds'?

Will it result in a 'pick and mix' style of Christianity, which gets the nod from the world but causes the heart of God to break?

I asked the Lord, 'What are the issues that will determine whether I give up, compromise, or become an overcomer?' There are many, but I will mention just three now, and many more we will pick up later on.

They are woven into the fabric of life, of our spiritual journey as well as our daily experience.

1. How will I react to the unexpected? (I never thought this could happen to me!)

This stops us in our tracks. It causes our mouth to drop open in disbelief. It leaves us stunned and even numbed. When it happens in our daily lives, and Covid impacted many of us severely, it is tough to handle. In our spiritual lives it can appear even harder, especially when the path Jesus wants us to travel on is not what we expected. In the case of the rich young ruler in Mark 10:17-27 it was the challenge to change his focus from financial gain and security to spiritual gain and eternity. It was too much for him; his initial motivation dissolved and died.

For the disciples in John 6 it was the unexpected realisation that Jesus was the Son of God, the bread of life, and his path demanded that they give up their own lives and follow him. It was too much for them, and their initial motivation dissolved and died, and they decided to go back to the comfortable and less challenging.

2. How will I react to the unfamiliar? (I never thought that the path once so clear could now become so unclear)

A familiar pattern and lifestyle is important to most of us. We feel safe, secure, comfortable and at peace. When either the lights dim, or the path narrows and enters a sudden direction never before anticipated, we find ourselves pressing the panic button or entering the fear zone. Spiritually, Jesus said that following him will feel like going down a narrow path. Our natural instinct tells us that this path is getting narrower and narrower and going nowhere. To make things worse, when we glance at the broad path it appears so attractive and progressive. The Israelites must have felt the same, wandering in the desert. It seemed so pointless; why not return to Egypt? 'After all, goodness knows where we are going or what will happen.'

Facing the giants, like Israel in Numbers 13:31-33, looks like nothing but a disaster. I have never been very courageous, and I think I never will be. Why not just give in and stay in the safe zone? What about those things outside of our understanding and experience that cause us to panic, fear and be afraid? Instead of looking up, we look down for man-made solutions, believing that God at best has turned his back on us, or at worst forsaken us. That initial motivation dissolves and dies.

3. How will I react to the unwanted? (I never thought that I would have to face things like this)

So much happened in the last two or three years that can certainly be classed as unwanted. Situations have had to be faced which before were not anticipated. We have all been affected in different ways. The rebound into our spiritual world has been just as tough. Some have received personal abuse and loss of friends for being a Christian. Others have had to face the possibility of losing their job because of their Christian principles. Current testing and trials on a Job-like scale, or at a lesser but equally painful level, have caught us off balance, that can leave us looking back rather than forward. Not to mention health challenges, marriage wobbles and doubts, serious financial difficulties, unexpected singleness and a host of other things which leave us crying out, 'Why me, Lord? It is not fair! After all I have tried to do for you, the Church and mission!'

How we handle these types of situations will determine whether resolution become reality, or motivation is turned into dedication and fulfilment.

Two thoughts immediately came to mind at this point. First, you must rely on truth, not feelings. Second, feelings must be shaped by truth, not emotion. If you want apostolic blessing you must have apostolic doctrine. Could it be true that we are more dominated by carnal reasoning than by spiritual truths? This fits into our postmodern world – if it feels OK, do it; if it doesn't, reject it.

> Watch your life and doctrine closely.
>
> (1 Timothy 4:16)

At this point I wrestled with two questions. What doctrinal truth will hold me together, and help me to make Jesus central, come what may? And what will enable me to be an overcomer and stay faithful to the end?

My aim is not to present a comprehensive answer, as it is beyond the brief of this book. But I will share one thought that seemed to me to be the spiritual glue to hold my life together at daunting times and challenges.

The Sovereignty of God (God is in control!)

Yes, over every single event that has taken and will take place in my life, both good and bad. Over all the sufferings of believers, and even though my feeble mind struggles to understand, my spirit tells me that God who is the Alpha and Omega is still with me.

> Dear friends, do not be surprised at the painful trial you are suffering, as though something strange were happening to you. But rejoice that you participate in the sufferings of Christ, so that you may be overjoyed when his glory is revealed.
>
> (1 Peter 4:12-13)

When my mind struggles, and the temptation to give up or believe that God no longer cares comes in full force, I turn to Job in the Old Testament, and take comfort and strength from his testimony. At the end of his life Job was purer in heart, humbler in spirit, clearer in vision, had increased in knowledge, was strengthened in faith, closer to God, restored in relationships and richer in blessings.

Can you hear Job say, 'I'm so glad I didn't give up on God when I faced the unexpected, the unfamiliar and the unwanted'?

God is in control. All the horrible things that have or will take place in my life, Satan means for evil, but God turns it for our good. I believe in God's central character, his goodness; that in his power and absolute authority, he is full of goodness and love, tender-hearted and compassionate towards me. I believe that all things that take place in my life will all work out for my good.[19] And, as we shall see later, nothing can be better than eternal life in the presence of God.

> Therefore, since we have a great high priest who has gone through the heavens, Jesus the Son of God, let us hold firmly to the faith we profess. For we do not have a high priest who is unable to sympathise with our weaknesses, but we have one who has been tempted in every way, just as we are – yet was without sin.
>
> (Hebrews 4:14-15)

The darkest time in history has to be when Jesus was nailed to the cross. The disciples, those closest to Jesus, were all totally baffled and confused. Satan and all his cohorts were rejoicing. In the middle of the day all went dark, but not in heaven. Scripture explains that at that moment all was going according to the Father's set plan. Hidden from human and even

19. See Romans 8:28.

demonic understanding, at the darkest point in history, God's perfect, eternal plan was being executed to the Father's glory and our salvation.

Let's finish this chapter with some promises of God.

> When you pass through the waters, I will be with you; and when you pass through the rivers, they will not sweep over you. When you walk through the fire, you will not be burned; the flames will not set you ablaze.
>
> (Isaiah 43:2-3)

> And we know that in all things God works for the good of those who love him, who have been called according to his purpose.
>
> (Romans 8:28)

> Never will I leave you; never will I forsake you.
>
> (Hebrews 13:5)

> Consider it pure joy, my brothers, whenever you face trials of many kinds, because you know that the testing of your faith develops perseverance. Perseverance must finish its work so that you may be mature and complete, not lacking anything.
>
> (James 1:2-4)

Responsibility does not come in glossy packaging

Years ago I heard a story of a police recruit taking an initiative test. When called to the scene he arrived to be jostled by a panic-stricken, nearly incoherent man. At the same time, a crowd was gathered around two other men clearly intent on killing each other. If this wasn't enough, behind them a burglar was obviously breaking into the house of one of the spectators. The panic-stricken man was now managing to say that his wife was about to give birth, and that the ambulance men were on strike, and his own car had broken down. The recruit could hardly take it in before he noticed across the street that a fire was rapidly spreading through a block of flats, and a woman was shouting for help from the top flat. When asked what to he should do in this situation, the recruit is alleged to have written, 'Take off uniform and mingle with the crowd.'[20]

We may smile, but the challenge in this preparatory stage of becoming an overcomer is clear. As we face the unexpected, the unfamiliar and the unwanted, will we take off our uniform of life in Christ and mingle with the crowd?

Some Questions

1. If God is calling you to be strong and courageous, what practical issues are you facing?
2. As you look at the end of Job's life, what inspiration do you draw from it for yourself personally?
3. What has been your track record to date of facing the unexpected, the unfamiliar and the unwanted? How have you responded? What have you learned from this?

---

20. Philip Greenslade, *Leadership: A Biblical Pattern for Today* (London: Marshall, Morgan and Scott, 1984). On page 27 he attributes first hearing 'the gist of this story from Gerald Coates'.

Chapter Six
The Journey: A Ride or a Race?

When we think of the Christian faith, what do we liken it to? More importantly, as we look through Scripture, how does it best describe the life of faith? It is, I believe, a crucial question, and how we answer it will reveal whether the topic of becoming an overcomer has any relevance to us.

When I read God's Word, and see his plan, purpose and desire for our lives, there is only one word to describe things: it is a journey. If the Bible is the greatest book on earth, then God's desire is that we experience and travel on the greatest journey anyone could travel on: from one extreme of being without hope and without God in this life, to the other of knowing him personally, seeing Him face to face and living with him eternally.

The life of faith is a journey

Throughout the whole Bible, the life of faith is seen as a journey. In Genesis 12 we read of Abraham stepping out in faith to leave a land of his ancestors and go to a place chosen by God. He did not know where he was going, but he knew who he would be travelling with, and who would be guiding and leading him. That was good enough for Abraham. Then we have the forty-year journey of the people of Israel from their harsh captivity and slavery in Egypt to the promised land of Canaan. Later we read of pilgrims setting out to travel to Jerusalem, Israel's historical capital, which was established around 1,000BC. In the heart of God's people Israel it has remained their capital ever since. After their exile in Babylon, we read of them journeying home to Jerusalem. In the New Testament the earliest term used to refer to Christians was those 'who belonged to the Way' (Acts 9:2). They were seen as travellers on their way to heaven.

The Pilgrim's Progress,[21] the much-loved Christian allegory written by John Bunyan, takes us on a journey from his home town, the City of Destruction, to the Celestial City, Heaven. Thinking of the Christian life as a journey through this world offers us a vivid and helpful way of visualising faith. It reminds us that we are going somewhere that God has prepared for us. It encourages us to look forward with anticipation to the complete joy that is to come. The goal is to arrive at our destination. I wonder how much of our time is spent thinking about our destination, as opposed to simply surviving the present. We shall see later how crucial and connected this is to overcoming.

How does Paul think of the Christian's journey – is it a ride or a race? How we answer this will determine whether we see overcoming as unnecessary or essential.

If it is a ride, I just get on and it takes me automatically to my destination. I can relax knowing that the conveyor belt of faith will take me automatically to my destination. Life is a breeze; I can relax.

If it is a race, then the life of faith takes on a totally different challenge. I need to train, prepare, sacrifice, have a plan and focus, embrace discipline and self-control, be patient, and most of all, persevere. At the same time, in the back of my mind I wonder, 'Will I finish the race or not?' Will I drop out through fatigue, or be tempted to give up? And will the opposition prove just too strong, forcing me to stop running? This is the context for the topic of an overcomer.

How does the apostle Paul see it?

21. John Bunyan, *The Pilgrim's Progress* (London: Penguin Classics, 2008).

> Do you not know that in a race all the runners run, but only one gets the prize? Run in such a way as to get the prize.
>
> (1 Corinthians 9:24)

I realised that Paul's focus was not just on effective ministry in the present – to see churches grow numerically, although that is always encouraging. The most successful churches to human eyes can be misleading, as with Sardis and Laodicea.[22] They looked the most successful and progressive, but did not receive approval from Jesus himself. So numbers, activities, progressive programmes and atmosphere are important, but Paul was looking beyond that. Paul's overarching calling was first for himself, and then those churches he had apostolic responsibility for. It was for him and them to receive, enter and finish the race, leading to the glory of eternal life with God. If his ministry meant anything, he was determined to be an example for all to follow. His heart was set on Christ.

> I have fought the good fight, I have finished the race, I have kept the faith. Now there is in store for me the crown of righteousness, which the Lord, the righteous Judge, will award to me on that day – and not only to me, but also to all who have longed for his appearing.
>
> (2 Timothy 4:7-8)

So for Paul the receiving of the crown was contingent on keeping the faith, running and finishing the race, and not a prize he received at the beginning of the race to be placed on his mantelpiece.

---

22. See Revelation 3.

A closer look at running the race

The context of running the race in 1 Corinthians 9:24-27 is Paul desiring to win the Jews and the Gentiles with the gospel. The race, the finish and prize refer to eternal life, and the receiving of the crown of righteousness. Paul's teaching is always double-edged, both for himself and for those listening to the gospel. His exhortation is to run the race in such a way as to win. For that to happen, strict training and discipline is required, fuelled by passion and purpose. Running will involve times of conflict and battle, as we have enemies and opposition determined to derail and disqualify us. This discipline and personal sacrifice Paul describes as beating the desires of the body into submission to Christ. The dominating thought in running the race is 'I must not be disqualified', and obviously Paul had this very much to the forefront of his mind too, as we see from verse 27. His goal was not to embrace a crippling fear, but to exhort and encourage us to not neglect the wonder of our salvation in Christ. Many spiritual problems occur through neglect, and particularly the Word of God and fellowship in the family of God.

Mo Farah

Mo Farah won the 5,000 and 10,000m at the London Olympic Games of 2012, and also at Rio in 2016. His training programme involved running up to 135 miles (217km) per week with no rest days, and two sessions every day but Sunday. It also included a vast amount of time away from his very close family, probably his greatest sacrifice.

What was his motivation through it all? He describes it as wanting to ensure that each of his four children had a gold medal of their own. He told *The Sun* newspaper that he just wanted to go home and see his family and hang the medals round the children's necks.[23]

23. www.thesun.co.uk/sport/Tokyo-olympics-2020/1647686/rio (accessed 22.6.22).

Mo Farah's race was anything but a ride – it was training, sacrifice, focus, passion, perseverance, learning through losing and so much more, and so is ours. However, our race is both similar and different to the Olympic races. In the Olympics only one person can win the race, but that is not true in ours. Some have not liked the comparison because of the competitive nature of running a race. We are not in competition with one another, and Paul by no means was implying that; in fact, just the opposite. If ever there was a man devoted to every believer running and finishing the race and receiving the prize, it was Paul. There are around sixty 'one another' references in the New Testament; Paul was certainly not advocating a selfish pursuit of the prize, but taught and demonstrated his passion of being an example and also an equipper and encourager for all to finish well. This is in fact the role and privilege of everyone in the body of Christ, the Church.

However, faith is individual and personal – it needs to be true for me, that truth transferred by the Spirit into my heart. Faith requires personal action and response, obedience birthed from a personal relationship with Jesus, and in that sense we run to 'get the prize' (v. 24).

Grace is the race

At this point Paul would remind us, just in case we begin to think too much of ourselves, that this is all of grace. In 1 Corinthians 15:10 he reminds the Church that it is 'by the grace of God I am what I am'. God's grace in him enabled him to work harder, labour, box, fight, run, discipline himself and be fruitful. What is the test? It is to ask ourselves this question: do we consider running the race as a part-time hobby, to stop and start at our convenience, or do we consider that running the race and finishing it is the consuming passion of our lives?

> Not that I have already obtained all of this, or have already been made perfect, but I press on to take hold of that for which Christ took hold of me. (Philippians 3:12)

Paul never lets us forget the gift of grace and faith in Ephesians 2. He then goes on in Ephesians 2:9 to say that salvation is 'not by works, so that no-one can boast'. How do these fit together when we talk about running the race? It would appear that we are focusing on our effort, ability and strength. It may be helpful at this point to look at James 2:17 – 'faith by itself, if it is not accompanied by action, is dead'. Are Paul and James contradicting each other? Understanding Paul's emphasis on faith and James on works will help us in running the race with our eyes fixed on Jesus.

Let's be clear that grace and faith are the means of salvation. Faith is not an intellectual quality by itself. It brings new life, it must express itself in practical everyday life, reflecting the goodness of God. By faith in Christ we are justified, it is the only way of being made right with God. However, the product of faith and justification is a life displaying trust and demonstrating the works of God. Faith justifies the man or woman before God, but works justifies the reality of faith in a man or woman by their actions. That is precisely the message James brings to us, and so does Paul. 'For we are God's workmanship, created in Christ Jesus to do good works, which God prepared in advance for us to do' (Ephesians 2:10). God is giving us through Paul and James two different angles on this critical issue so that we get it in balance. This will enable us to rest in our salvation and pick up the baton and run the race. Active faith is our responsible response (works) to the unmerited grace of God.[24]

Therefore, run to win the prize. Run looking to Jesus, the 'author

24. See Romans 12:1.

and finisher of our faith' (Hebrews 12:2, RSV). Run the race; don't just sit in the stands and watch. Run to glorify God. Run, as Hebrews 12:1 instructs, 'with perseverance'. Never flag or drop out of the race, but run with focus and purpose; serve and glorify God. As we keep ourselves in the love of God, he will 'keep [us] from falling', and enable us to finish the race (Jude 21,24).

In finishing this chapter Paul brings this challenge to himself:

> that… I myself will not be disqualified …
> (1 Corinthians 9:27)

If anyone should not have to say this it is surely the apostle Paul, but he does say it!

> So, if you think you are standing firm, be careful that you don't fall!
> (1 Corinthians 10:12)

Why? Because your enemies – the world, flesh and Satan – are working for your downfall, so that you leave the life of faith and stop running the race. This is Paul at the end of his life, determined that we shall all keep our names in the Lamb's book of life – but more about that later.

Some Questions

1. Are you running the race, or are you currently wanting an easy ride? What are some of your personal temptations to choose an easy ride? What spurs you on to run the race?
2. If you are in the race, what does it mean for you to prepare, sacrifice, embrace discipline and self-control, and be patient?

3. Which of these two questions are you asking, and why? 'What is the least I need to do and still be a Christian?' or 'What behaviour will maximise my zeal for God and his kingdom?'

Chapter Seven
If Life is a Journey, Does That Mean Salvation is a Journey Too?

From previous chapters we have seen that salvation originates in the love, grace and mercy of God. Its saving power is the blood of Christ, and it takes effect in our lives by the truth of the Word of God and the ministry of the Holy Spirit, who opens our eyes and our hearts. The entry point to salvation is repentance and faith.

The apostle Paul is a great help to us at this point, and his teaching is fundamental to our understanding, both of the wonder of this moment and the challenging journey it puts us on. Paul teaches salvation as a journey, as we shall see in the following verses.

> [He] *has saved us* and called us to a holy life – not because of anything we have done but because of his own purpose and grace. This grace was given us in Christ Jesus before the beginning of time ...
>
> (2 Timothy 1:9, my emphasis)

Some of us can remember the moment when our lives changed through faith in Jesus. My own story, as shared earlier, became a Christmas like no other. Like the shepherds in Luke 2:8-20, my dark world was flooded with the light and truth of the gospel, and for the first time I felt loved, forgiven, clean and in a different world – a child of the kingdom of God. But this was just the beginning and not the end of the journey. It continues, and Paul reminds us of that:

> For the message of the cross is foolishness to those who are perishing, but to us who are *being saved* it is the power of God.
>
> (1 Corinthians 1:18, my emphasis)

Whilst I was so grateful to Jesus for his gift of life and salvation, I soon became aware, and that is still the same today, of the 'much more' that I need to understand of God's Word, receive of his love, grace and mercy, and allow the Spirit of God to continue his life-transforming work in my life. I may be further on that I was at the beginning some forty-eight years ago, but I am still not at the end of the journey… it continues.

> Since we have now been justified by his blood, how much more *shall we be saved* from God's wrath through him!
>
> (Romans 5:9, my emphasis)

So salvation has a past, a present, and this verse points to a future aspect. Our complete salvation is future, when we are finally set free from the presence of sin, and when the last enemy – death – has been conquered.[25] But this is still to come, and will require extreme diligence, faith, courage and perseverance – yes, be an overcomer!

It may be helpful to see the way that Paul writes to the Romans and takes what I have just shared about the journey of salvation, using more theological terms. But Paul's intention is not to educate in a lecture or seminar setting, but to be intensely practical, down to earth and relevant to every single person. Paul teaches about this journey and we may be able to identify and reflect upon this in our own lives past, present and indeed our desired future.

25. See Revelation 20:14.

Condemnation

It begins for all of us in a place of separation from Christ. Salvation in Christ is not the need of a few wayward and evil people. All people need to be rescued. 'There is no-one righteous, not even one' (Romans 3:10). The need is universal, 'for all have sinned and fall short of the glory of God' (Romans 3:23). Salvation for both Jews and Gentiles is founded not on human achievement but on God's grace and Christ's sacrificial death.

Justification

We have already mentioned justification by faith. It is when God sets us free from the penalty of sin, which is the result of our broken relationship with him. He declares that we are right with him, made possible through the redeeming work of Jesus. It is an amazing moment when by the Spirit we hear these words from Romans 8:1: 'Therefore, there is now no condemnation for those who are in Christ Jesus'. God has judged our case early and found us righteous because our lives are 'now hidden with Christ in God' (Colossians 3:3).

Sanctification

Having been set free from the penalty of sin, our lives need so much cleaning. The power of sin has been broken, and the continuing work of the Word and the Spirit sets us free so that we can be constantly changed from 'one degree of glory to another' (2 Corinthians 3:18, RSV). Sanctification is a process, because sin still remains in our lives, but our desire for obedience as a child of God brings us to this place of consecration, as Romans 12:1-2 teaches.

Glorification

… is the final stage in God's work of salvation. It is the crowning achievement of sanctification, in which Christians are fully conformed to the image of Christ. It is receiving that new body, rejoined with soul and spirit in resurrection, to live in a universe restored to its original state.

This journey takes us from the very depth of despair to the very height of glory and wonder. However, in the day-to-day issues we all face comes the realisation that the journey can be slowed up or stopped.

As we draw this chapter to a close, we reaffirm that the gospel is the 'way of salvation' along which we need to travel to reach our destination. It is neither an instant event nor a convenient and pleasant ride, but a race that we need to run. It is a race we can grow tired of and give up on, a race that we can be tempted to pull out of and be disqualified from, as Paul mentions in 1 Corinthians 9:27. Therefore, being an overcomer, or as Paul puts it in Romans 8:37 'more than [a conqueror]', is crucial.

The process of being slowed down, stopped or tempted to return to the old ways is commonly known as 'backsliding'. The danger is that when this is mentioned we make a general statement: 'Well, everybody does it.' Whilst that may be true it does not make it normal, or minimise the potential danger of treating it as so. We do not dwell on the past, but we need to learn from it. Why did this happen? How did God bring me through? How can I protect myself from repeating yesterday's mistakes? As I have looked at my own life I have identified some causes.

The focus of my heart changed from God to the world. Paul tells us that 'the god of this age' blinds our eyes to the truth (2 Corinthians 4:4).

'I' becomes the centre, as in Philippians 2:21: 'For everyone looks out for his own interests, not those of Jesus Christ.'

Listening and obeying the voice of the Spirit becomes less important, hence the challenge in Revelation: 'He who has an ear, let him hear what the Spirit says' (Revelation 2:7,11,17,29; 3:6,13,22).

Reading the Word becomes more of a struggle, the subtle tempting of Satan in Genesis 3:1: 'Did God really say…?'

Suddenly self-importance takes number one slot; pride and self-confidence lead to the tolerance of sin. 'Do not follow the crowd in doing wrong' (Exodus 23:2). The slippery slope at first seems so innocuous, but it can finish up with our denying the faith.

We will mention more of this battle later, but there are two powers at work: one to move you forward (the Spirit) and one to take you back (the flesh). Paul in true apostolic fashion urges us all to 'press on' (Philippians 3:14). As Christians we have a choice: to choose the Spirit or the flesh. Paul's desire is that the glory that is to come becomes so illumined by the Spirit that we will hold on and not let go. We persevere and walk in the Spirit right to the very last day of our lives.

As I read the New Testament I see no alternative. Paul does not give us an easy path to glory. There is no shortcut from justification to glorification missing out sanctification. Faith in Jesus is not a stop-start, New Year resolution kind of response. The words 'faith' and 'faithfulness' in the Greek and Hebrew are the same, as I mentioned earlier. To trust in someone is to keep on trusting them, no matter what may occur. The verb 'believe' is often in the present tense, referring to a continual action.

Paul picks this up from Habakkuk 2:4 that 'The righteous will live [and keep on living] by his faith'.

> For in the gospel the righteousness from God is revealed, a righteousness that is by faith from first to last, just as it is written: 'The righteous will live by faith.'
>
> (Romans 1:17)

As we have mentioned before, for Paul the triumph is that he has kept the faith right to the very end, as we read in 2 Timothy 4:7, and he exhorts Timothy and thereby you and me to follow his example.

True faith is the faith that we finish with, not what we start with. Faith is therefore a walk into the next life, and not an eternal insurance policy that gives us the freedom to live as we like in the present day.

Jesus spoke into this situation in John 15:4: 'Remain in me, and I will remain in you.' In other words, eternal life is not so much a possession as a position in Christ. Genuine assurance of eternal life comes not from clinging to a memory of the past, but by seeing the Holy Spirit's continuing, transforming work on our lives – yes, being a disciple to the very end of life.

Remember:

Faith, like grace, is not static; saving faith is more than understanding the facts; it is inseparable from repentance, surrender and supernatural eagerness to obey.

Why are we eager to obey? Because we have seen that Jesus is both Saviour and Lord. This we now 'confess with [our] mouth' and 'believe in [our] heart' (Romans 10:9). It is the supreme work of the Holy Spirit. All that took place in Acts 2 – the tongues of fire, the worship, Peter's preaching, the 3,000 new believers and the remarkable daily fellowship together – points to one supreme truth, that Jesus is 'both Lord and Christ' (Acts 2:36). When this is revealed to our hearts there is that flutter of amazement, excitement and joy that cements a godly determination to be faithful, hold on and persevere to our final day, because then joy unspeakable will be ours. We shall be with Jesus forever, but we are not there yet! This leads us to the next chapter, and a deeper understanding of discipleship.

Some questions

1. Sanctification is the work of the Spirit taking place now in all of us. Identify some of the current issues you are facing.
2. In what areas is God seeking to move you forward so that your faith grows and matures?
3. If Jesus is both Saviour and Lord, review how this is expressed in your daily life and service.

Chapter Eight
Jesus' Call to Discipleship

In Chapters Three and Four we looked at the transition from believer to disciple. The Holy Spirit brings us to realise our absolute, desperate need of God, showing us hope and also the starting point of our journey – repentance and faith in Jesus. We have seen that this is not the end of the journey but the beginning of a new life as a disciple. Eternal life is a gift, but discipleship is a costly journey, and it is Jesus' express command that we become and also 'make disciples' (Matthew 28:18-20).

After his resurrection, with the authority that is his, he instructed the eleven disciples – and thereby you and me – to go and 'make disciples of all nations'. As we follow in obedience to his commands and depend on the Holy Spirit to lead, guide, inspire and anoint, then Jesus promises his presence will remain with us until the 'end of the age'.

Discipleship is all about following Jesus. This means following and imitating things that he said and things that he did. This is how Luke introduces Acts 1. Acts is a reflection of Jesus' life and ministry through redeemed men and women anointed by the Holy Spirit. There should not be a difference between believing and following Jesus, but unfortunately, as we are only too aware, there often *is* a difference. The Gospel writers make it clear that when Jesus called Peter, James, John and the others it was to believe in him[26] but also to follow him.[27] Jesus himself gives the challenge, 'follow me' (Matthew 4:19). This involves the mind (believing), but also action and lifestyle.[28] It was to consider every other issue secondary to following Jesus.

26. See John 1:12.
27. See Matthew 16:24.
28. See Mark 1:17-18.

The question must be, 'What does discipleship look like, and do our lives match this?'

Definition of a disciple

Many attribute the meaning of disciple to Herodotus, nearly 500 years before Jesus walked on this earth. He referred to a disciple as a learner or apprentice. The Greek word *mathetos* means 'one who learns instruction from another'. So in Jesus' time it was used in this way, an apprentice to a tradesman, one who learns and then imitates, and as a carpenter Jesus would have understood this.

While classroom teaching and learning is part of the discipleship process, it is only the first part. A student who never progressed past the classroom would not be considered a disciple. Of course learning was important, but it had to be followed by putting into practice, demonstrating that which had been learned.

This was Jesus' pattern with his disciples. He taught them, showed them what it was to 'preach good news to the poor', 'proclaim freedom for the prisoners', see the blind get their sight back, 'release the oppressed', and 'proclaim the year of the Lord's favour'. This meant freedom from sin and its consequences (Luke 4:18-19), and 'healing every disease and sickness' (Matthew 9:35). He then 'gave them authority to drive out evil spirits and to heal every disease and sickness' (Matthew 10:1), and even 'raise the dead' (Matthew 10:8). Then he sent them out, telling them that the fields are 'ripe for harvest' (John 4:35).

The disciples learned by listening, seeing and then doing. Matthew 4:19 makes this clear when Jesus says, 'Come, follow me … and I will make you fishers of men.' Here are the three essential elements of a disciple.

'Come, follow me' – there is no alternative option. It requires being so convinced of who Jesus is that no matter what trials, persecution and hardships we may face, or how the coming years may pan out, we will go on believing and following.

'I will make you' – Isaiah 41:14-15 brings the word from the Lord, how the feeble and despised will be helped supernaturally by God himself to be a sharp instrument of harvest:

> 'Do not be afraid, O worm Jacob, O little Israel, for I myself will help you,' declares the LORD, your Redeemer, the Holy One of Israel. 'See, I will make you into a threshing-sledge, new and sharp, with many teeth. You will thresh the mountains and crush them, and reduce the hills to chaff.'

Now Jesus, commissioned by the Father and anointed by the Holy Spirit, completes that promise to all of his disciples.

'Fishers of men' reveals how incredible a miracle this is. It means becoming something that is completely impossible except by the grace, mercy, redeeming love and power of God. What greater privilege in life can there be than to so influence and impact a person through the gospel that they too repent and believe that Jesus is the Christ, the Son of the living God.

Learning language in Bangkok

I arrived in Bangkok on 10 February 1978. My one aim was to be able to read, write and speak the Thai language to the best of my ability. Little did I know what a humbling experience this would be, but at the same time such a privilege. I managed to get a room in a hostel not too far from my language school. After several months I was able to communicate in a broken way, and was constantly trying my new language out on anyone who would listen, much to their amusement and my embarrassment.

After nine months I managed to pass the basic government language exam. My helper was a young Thai man who worked as a night guard at my hostel. He loved to sing, and I played the guitar and introduced him to some Thai Christian songs. Through this the Lord began to work in his heart, and together we started reading the Gospels on a regular basis. I will never forget this very first young man who came to believe in Jesus, and who later was baptised in the local church. 'A fisher of men' – the thought still brings tears to my eyes.

Will some disciples turn back?

We are coming to a point where life can get uncomfortable. The Holy Spirit desires to move us along into a greater understanding and experience of the salvation that is in Jesus Christ and in him alone. Our eyes have been opened to the cost of discipleship, realising that to walk in newness of life will be challenged more and more the further we go on this journey. It is a phase of the journey equivalent to 'hitting the wall' in marathon terms. For the marathon runner, the wall is the point at which you run out of energy, where it feels like you can't go on. Runners speak about a sudden wave of fatigue that sets in at about twenty miles into a marathon. It is a critical point in the race, both for the elite runner like Mo Farah and the occasional jogger. It is often the point where the decision is made, either to call it a day and just be thankful you managed to get so far, or to press on and finish the race at all costs.

When reading the book of Revelation, I noticed that the word 'disciple' does not occur. 'Discipline' is mentioned in Revelation 3:19, but not 'disciple'; it is replaced by 'overcomer'. (In other translations the Greek word *nikao* is translated slightly differently, but with the same meaning: for example, 'the one who is victorious', in Revelation 2:7 – NIV 2011; or 'the one who conquers' – ESV.) We will pick up on this in a later chapter. Therefore the question I began asking myself was, 'Will I be a disciple who becomes an overcomer?'

Jesus' challenge in John 6

John 6 helps us to understand this challenge. He tells us of Jesus feeding the 5,000 with five small loaves and two fish. In the evening his disciples attempted to cross the lake to Capernaum in an impossible storm, and John recounts how Jesus came walking towards them on the water. Later Jesus then spoke to the crowds following him:

> I tell you the truth, you are looking for me, not because you saw miraculous signs but because you ate the loaves and had your fill. (John 6:26)

Miracles in John's Gospel are called 'signs' for a very good reason. Their supreme aim is to show who Jesus really is, and John makes this abundantly clear in his Gospel. 'I am the bread of life' … 'I am the light of the world' … 'I am the door' (ESV) or 'gate' … 'I am the good shepherd' … 'I am the resurrection and the life' … 'I am the way and the truth and the life' ... 'I am the true vine' (John 6:35; John 8:12; John 10:7-9; John 10:14-15; John 11:25-26; John 14:16; John 15:1-2).

In John 6 the focus is on Jesus the bread of life. The crowd were content to follow Jesus up to this point, but began to feel uneasy when they realised what Jesus was saying about himself. He is the Christ, the very source of life itself, claiming His divinity and pre-existence before coming to earth. The internal battle raging at this moment becomes clear. If they acknowledge and believe who Jesus says he is, then they have no option but to surrender their lives to him in repentance and faith, and become disciples and overcomers.

What response did Jesus get?

> This is a hard teaching. Who can accept it?
> (John 6:60)

Somewhere deep inside all of us is the hope that following Jesus is not as costly and demanding as he said it is, secretly wishing that the narrow road will widen out and mix with the broad road and bring back a little normality! How many times have I pondered over this! And yet the Holy Spirit reminds me of the truth that the cross is central to salvation and discipleship. When Jesus said, 'take up [your] cross and follow me' (Matthew 16:24), there is no optional 'get-out clause' giving us permission to rejoin the broad way for a bit of relaxation and a change.

The privilege and joy of serving as a missionary in Asia for more than forty years is incalculable, and yet there have been some moments of pain and heartache. There was the joy of seeing people genuinely believe and give testimony to the life-changing salvation that Jesus had given them, and having the courage and commitment to become part of the church, often facing much criticism. That joy turned to sorrow as some, many years later and under severe pressure, returned to the temple and their former Buddhist ways. This challenge comes to all of us. Even missionaries who have left home and travelled to different parts of the world, learned the language and with passion preached the gospel and seen small groups of believers form communities of faith have not all continued to believe and follow. I am reminded that past service is no guarantee of future faithfulness.

> From this time many of his disciples turned back and no longer followed him. (John 6:66)

Paul the apostle experienced this heartache and pain too. In 2 Timothy 4:10 he writes about Demas, a fellow worker and dear friend[29] who deserted him because of his love for the world. This is the reality of these last days, as Jesus teaches in Matthew 24:9-14. Opposition to our Christian faith and lifestyle will increase, as will persecution. With the increase of false prophets, deception will be at an all-time high. The result will be that love for Christ will cool and morals will be compromised, resulting in many turning away from their faith. At the same time, on a positive note, despite these difficult and testing last days, there will be those who rise up with a new anointing of the Spirit, stand firm, and take up the commission given by Jesus, taking the gospel to every tribe, tongue and nation. It is time to emulate Simon Peter, who responded to Jesus' question in John 6:67, 'You do not want to leave too, do you?', with:

> 'Lord, to whom shall we go? You have the words of eternal life. We believe and know that you are the Holy One of God.'
>
> (John 6:68-69)

The book of Acts is seen as the goal for churches today: the amazing power of the Spirit bringing numerical growth and geographical advance, mighty miracles and astonishing encounters through the Holy Spirit. This is right, and the COVID-19 pandemic has made many of us aware of our desperate need of a new anointing of the Spirit to demonstrate the love, grace, mercy and power of salvation that is in Jesus. But also woven through its story is martyrdom, persecution, imprisonment and incredible suffering because of the gospel, and the disciples' committed lifestyle to take the gospel from Jerusalem to Judea, Samaria 'and to the ends of the earth' (Acts 1:8).

29. See Philemon 24; Colossians 4:14.

Throughout the pages of the New Testament you will find this: 'endure hardship'; 'be patient in endurance; stand 'firm to the end'; 'remain in me'; be resolute in heart… be 'steadfast' and immovable; 'resist', be firm in your faith; persevere in all trials; 'do not be surprised at [these] painful trial[s]'; 'be strong in the Lord'; 'count it all joy' whenever you face trials and testing (2 Timothy 4:5; Colossians 1:11; Matthew 10:22; John 15:4; 1 Peter 5:10; 1 Peter 5:9; James 1:3; 1 Peter 4:12; Ephesians 6:10; James 1:2, KJV). And these reach a peak in Revelation 3:11: 'Hold on to what you have, so that no-one will take your crown.'

There is no need for anyone to turn back. If the Father, Son and Holy Spirit are for us, who can be against us – except ourselves? We are saved by grace (the works of Jesus, not ours) through faith, continued and persistent. Forgiveness is given to those who go on believing.[30] Holiness, without which 'no-one will see the Lord' (Hebrews 12:14), is given to those who go on believing as they continue to trust and obey. God is then able to complete the work he has begun in us. 'His divine power has given us everything we need for life and godliness' (2 Peter 1:3)

Paul, Peter and John were not just trying to scare us into submission to Christ; they were being faithful to the Holy Spirit in bringing truth that did not just apply to their first-century challenge, but to every century and to every disciple, including you and me today.

Jesus himself sounded the warning:

> I am sending you out like sheep among wolves.
>
> (Matthew 10:16)

30. See 1 John 1:9.

> 'No servant is greater than his master.' If they persecuted me, they will persecute you also.
>
> (John 15:20)

Matthew 24:9-14 makes us face up to these last days, when believers will be hated for their faith in Jesus; the difference between genuine and nominal Christians will become clear; 'the love of most will grow cold', and faith in Jesus will be compromised.

Will the fear of people win the day, or the fear of God? The challenge is clear… get ready now!

Jesus also brought encouragement and hope. He has made provision for this time by giving us the Holy Spirit. In John 14-16 He promised the Holy Spirit, the Comforter, the same Spirit that would raise him from the dead, and will raise us too.[31]

> I have told you these things, so that in me you may have peace. In this world you will have trouble. But take heart! I have overcome the world.
>
> (John 16:33)

As we approach the next chapter, the scales, at present delicately balanced, now begin to move in favour of overcoming as we understand and embrace all that this entails.

We finish this chapter referring back to John 6, when Jesus, after seeing many disciples turning away, asked his disciples, 'You do not want to leave too, do you?' Our positive response, like Peter's, will take us into the next chapter and our focus of overcoming.

31. See Romans 8:11.

Some Questions

1. We have looked at what discipleship is. As you reflect on this, what corresponds with your life now – and what doesn't?
2. We mentioned earlier phrases like:

'endure hardship'; 'be patient in endurance; stand 'firm to the end'; 'remain in me'; be resolute in heart… be 'steadfast' and immovable; 'resist', be firm in your faith; persevere in all trials; 'do not be surprised at [these] painful trial[s]'; 'be strong in the Lord'; 'count it all joy' whenever you face trials and testing.

Are any of these relevant to you now? Be specific.

3. A disciple is always looking to encourage and help others. Who is close to you? Share some of this content with them, and pray for them.

Chapter Nine
Discipleship and the First Glimpse of Overcoming

Many of us will either have read about, or seen through films or documentaries, the competitive world of the ancient Greek and Roman world. The Greek word *nikao* denotes a victor, a champion, or one who possesses some type of superiority over another. The Greeks loved the word *nike*. They actually had a goddess by the name Nike. She was the goddess of victory, the goddess of triumph, and the Greeks actually believed that victory could not be achieved by humans, but only by gods! The two main victories represented at this time are 1) an athlete who was a supreme champion in their sport; and 2) a military victory of one enemy over the other. Therefore the word means to conquer, to defeat, to master, to overcome, to overwhelm, to surpass, or to be victorious.

With the ancient background of only the gods giving victory, it reinforces the truth that the Christian's ability to conquer and be a winner is only due to Christ's power living in and through them.

Two familiar passages of Scripture come to mind at this point.

In John 16:33 Jesus himself uses the verb form when he says, 'In this world you will have trouble. But take heart! I have overcome the world.'

In Romans 8:35 Paul asks the question, can anything 'separate us from the love of Christ?', and his swift reply is in verse 37: 'No, in all these things we are more than conquerors through him who loved us.' Paul is in fact saying that we are not just *nike* (conquerors), but we are *hyper-nike* (super-conquerors). In fact, nothing that we can possibly face, even death itself, can separate us from Christ Jesus, our Lord (v.39).

So let's recap. When the word *nikao* is used in Scripture it was conveying two messages.

First, the only way for believers to defeat the enemy they face is for them to maintain the attitude of an athlete. We have already mentioned this in Chapter Six. To have a winning focus we will need to eliminate all spiritual apathy, and prepare for the toughest competition ever engaged in. Nothing less than a full commitment and determination to win the race will be sufficient to master the exterior adversaries and interior struggles we all will face. Whether this imagery referred to a runner, wrestler, discus thrower, or any other type of first-century athlete, the New Testament message is clear: only a thoroughly committed believer will win a victor's crown.

Second, the word *nikao* was also used militarily, and the calling of the Church is to rise up like an army to attack and defeat the external and internal enemies that threaten it. Paul teaches the Ephesian church to put on 'the full armour of God' (Ephesians 6:11). Spiritual complacency will be like the termites I referred to earlier, bringing destruction and defeat. Apathy and complacency are always the most difficult enemies for a person or a church to conquer.

It is important at this stage to remind ourselves that the tense for 'overcoming' speaks of a continuous and ongoing victory. This means that Christ wasn't urging believers to run a temporary race or to fight a short-term battle. He was demanding a commitment to start and to remain in the race until they reached the finish line — to attack and defeat their foes, and to remain victorious over their enemies. Jesus was actually asking them, as he asks each of us, to be permanently and consistently undeterred in overcoming and obtaining victory in every area of their lives. Christians in every generation are to make it their continual and unrelenting goal to maintain victory in every possible sphere of life as long as they live on this earth.

Overview of an overcomer

To be an overcomer is to grow into another level of discipleship; not only to follow, but to be steadfast and endure trials. It is to resist the power and temptations that Satan and the world present; to hold fast to Christ right to the end, the very last breath, refusing to turn away when difficult times and persecution come; to have complete dependence upon God for direction, purpose, fulfilment and strength to follow and live out his plan for our lives, and to accept the high cost of discipleship, even to the point of being hated for the sake of Christ.[32]

The essence of being an overcomer is loyal, faithful obedience.

This loyal, faithful obedience will be tested. Revelation 7:14 speaks about the 'great tribulation', a period of final hostility prior to Christ's return. Whilst there are various views on this, few would disagree that there is a build-up of increasing anti-Christian behaviour in our rapidly changing world. That many will pay the price with their own blood, and that the number of martyrs is increasing year on year, is beyond doubt. The early Church considered this an honour, as does the Chinese Church today. The word 'martyr' is almost synonymous with the word 'witness', and is wholeheartedly embraced and taught in the Alpha course[33] material in China. In the West we would be afraid to do this, as it might put off those seeking to know Jesus. But the approach in China seems to follow the teaching of Jesus. Knowing and following Jesus will require a purposeful, determined, unwavering, single-minded and steadfast decision to put him first. Self-denial is not the same as denial of self. Self-denial can still mean that the denial is actually *for* me, my self-promotion and honour. In that sense, self in the Bible is humanity acting independently of God for their own glory and benefit.

32. See Mark 13:13.

33. An Alpha course seeks to introduce the basics of the Christian faith through a series of talks and discussions. See https://alpha.org.uk/ (accessed 22.6.22).

However, denial of self is completely the opposite. It is best seen in Paul's statement in Philippians 1:21, 'For to me, to live is Christ and to die is gain.' In denying self, Paul has only one goal: that Christ may be glorified in every aspect of his life, and he has no shred of desire to promote self in any way. In Romans 9:3 he says, 'For I could wish that I myself were cursed and cut off from Christ for the sake of my brothers'. What an astonishing Christ-like statement of love for his fellow Jews – that is truly the denial of self.

> … anyone who does not take his cross and follow me is not worthy of me. (Matthew 10:38)

> If anyone is ashamed of me and my words in this adulterous and sinful generation, the Son of Man will be ashamed of him when he comes in his Father's glory with the holy angels.
>
> (Mark 8:38)

The decision we make today is an eternal decision and determines our future. The life of tomorrow is offered to us here and now.

Persecution seems unnatural to us in the West, but in China and many other persecuted places it is an inevitable consequence of believing in Jesus. Let's just reflect on the attitude of the Chinese Church towards persecution.

When they are persecuted, they do not hate the government or whoever is persecuting them, but accept punishment as unto the Lord and for the privilege of suffering in his name. They endure silently, praying as Jesus instructed, for their enemies.[34] When leaders or believers are persecuted

34. See Matthew 5:45.

and sent to labour camps, they do not complain. They still love their country, waiting for God to grant their nation mercy. They execute their duties diligently, and detention centres hold believers in high regard. They live out their Christian faith with determination and joy, knowing that their faith is not in vain; they will enjoy the presence of the Lord both now and forever.

As we approach the next chapter, the challenge of being an overcomer is gradually sharpening its focus. Entering and living in the kingdom requires no hesitation; it is a costly and radical decision requiring much courage. The rich young ruler in Matthew 19:16-22 had a deep desire to find eternal life, but the challenge to turn about, leave the old life, and receive new life in Jesus and follow him was too much. Having riches was not the obstacle, and does not preclude discipleship, but yielding all this to God does! The kingdom is not to bring people into poverty, but to deliver them from false security. The life of tomorrow is offered to us here and now, and we can't hold onto what we have left behind.

Some Questions

1. Reflect personally on the journey so far. What has impacted you, and why?
2. Taking the first few words of Philippians 1:21; expand on 'For to me, to live …' in a personal, up-to-date statement.

Chapter Ten
Preparing the Way to Overcome – Hezekiah, Isaiah and Us!

At this moment two questions come to the surface:

1. How can we endure persecution and suffering for Jesus?
2. How did the Old Testament prophets, and the apostles Paul and John, endure?

Before we have a closer look at these questions, let's first look at the book of Revelation. Revelation is full of promises and warnings. This last book in the Bible is addressed to believers about to face a huge test of faith, with the intention for them and us to come through with flying colours. We hold on to Jesus' words from Matthew 24:13: 'he who stands firm to the end will be saved', and the corresponding verse in Revelation 3:11: 'Hold on to what you have, so that no-one will take your crown.'

In order to get ready, we need to know the challenge before us: it is to endure to the end. If we are to endure and hold on to the end, where do we start? Revelation 1-3 gives us the starting point, and hence this chapter. Prepare now for tomorrow! Get ready! The theme 'Prepare the way of the Lord' runs through many portions of Scripture both in the Old and New Testaments. We will pick this up later, but for now let's learn from Hezekiah and Isaiah from the Old Testament. How did they prepare? What were their struggles? What lessons can we learn from them?

Hezekiah

Hezekiah came to the throne at one of the darkest moments in Judah's history. His father, Ahaz, was a failure as a king. He was wicked, and destroyed the nation's belief in God. Dark as this time was, it was also a time to experience change and see a nation revived. 2 Chronicles 29 tells us what Hezekiah did. He took responsibility, and followed through on what his heart had learned about God. He prepared the way for the Lord. How?

He unlocked the Temple doors and repaired them. He gathered all the priests and Levites together in order to do three things: consecrate themselves to the Lord, consecrate the Temple to the Lord, and make a covenant with the Lord.

This was God's starting point, and Hezekiah prepared the way for the Lord to bring revival. It doesn't matter what the world thinks. It doesn't matter if the world ridicules and opposes. It doesn't matter how inferior or inadequate we may feel. It doesn't matter how remote and unlikely any change may seem. The prophetic word comes through powerfully at these testing, difficult and often painful times:

> … do not be negligent now, for the Lord has chosen you to stand before him and serve him, to minister before him …
>
> (2 Chronicles 29:11)

Imitate Hezekiah! Seize the moment and give God a chance to do a miracle! Do not sit on the fence or wait for a more convenient time. Open the door of your heart (the temple, the place of worship) for the Spirit to do a new thing. Consecrate yourself to walk, grow and serve in God's way. Put yourself in that place where God's blessing can come upon you. Make a covenant with the Lord: 'I will not be negligent; I will stand before you; I will serve and minister to you, and give you an invitation to work in and through me in a way that glorifies God alone.'

What other things can we learn from Hezekiah in how he prepared the way which may be helpful to us today? Two things come to mind which are practical and foundational.

1. He allowed someone to speak into his life

There is every reason to believe that Isaiah had become a prophetic pastor to this young man, as he had access into the palace. There seems little other explanation. He was the prophet to the nation. There is every likelihood that Hezekiah allowed his heart to be stirred by Isaiah's testimony in Isaiah 6. Isaiah's faith and commitment to God's calling and vision birthed something in Hezekiah's heart too as he listened to the way God had worked, spoken to, changed and challenged Isaiah's life. He was given a vision, and through this he allowed the Spirit of God to touch his heart. He believed God at the darkest hour. When it was God's time, he acted with immediate obedience; he was ready for God's moment!

There is a clear lesson here for me and for all of us… We need someone to speak into our lives, someone who will hear God's prophetic word for us. We need someone who has the courage to speak that word, and a heart to mentor and model God to our lives. We need someone who has the ability to draw our heart to God's, and will lay their life down for us! Someone to be accountable to, with whom we can be honest, knowing that what we share is safe.

Hezekiah would have found Isaiah to be that crucial, God-given gift to prepare him for the coming challenge.

2. He treasured, protected and fed upon God's vision until God's moment arrived

Living in that evil palace environment, you can imagine the many temptations and challenges for him to give up. 'The forces against you are just too many; the dream is good, but you will get over it in a few weeks, and wake up to the reality that nothing is going to change!'

Story of China and back to Jerusalem

Mark Ma, a dedicated Christian, was born in the Henan Province. In 1942 while praying he heard God challenge him to go into Xinjiang – a region of China – and to preach the gospel. This was a Muslim-dominated area. Five months later, he met two others who earlier had received the same call. Soon there were eight students burdened for Xinjiang. But God was going to widen the vision beyond Xinjiang to Jerusalem!

At the turn of the twentieth century revival came to parts of China. The fire of the Spirit burned strongly in the Church, who took upon themselves Jesus' words in Acts 1:8. The vision, received from God, was to take the Good News to the unreached nations to the west of China, going back across Asia all the way to Jerusalem, where the Church started. (The Chinese call this missionary movement 'Back to Jerusalem'. As they had been so blessed by the sacrifice of many bringing the gospel to China, so they now see their calling to take the gospel back to Jerusalem – yes, to every needy person and nation.)

In March 1947, two men and five women set out to Xinjiang. It was a very dangerous journey, together with much opposition. However, political developments and strict government officials prevented them from continuing on their journey. It appeared to be another example of the unexpected and unwanted seemingly blocking the vision. Did they give in? No! God had given them a vision. He is faithful.

Simon Zhao picked up this vision. Born on 1 June 1918, Simon Zhao, whose name was Zhao Haizhen, was born in Shenyang in Liaoning Province in north-east China. Tragically his father died when he was still young and his godly mother was forced to raise the children single-handedly. His heart was bitter through these difficult years but eventually he gave his life to God. Sometime later, as he was praying, the Lord gave Simon a vision of the north-west province of Xinjiang.

In 1948 he arrived with his team in Kashgar, an oasis city in the Tarim Basin region of southern Xinjiang. Very soon all his team were arrested, imprisoned, and only Simon came out alive, and that after more than forty years in prison. The vision appeared to die. Despite incredibly dark times during the Cultural Revolution, Simon, Mark and others continued to pray that a new generation of Chinese believers would complete the vision. If ever there was an illustration of motivation turning into dedication and accomplishment it was seen in the incredibly turbulent years of this movement.

As we look back now, we see a Chinese Church of 100 million-plus Christians, and tens of thousands involved in taking the gospel to the unreached. They are today fulfilling the vision given by God eighty years ago.[35]

As I reflect on this, the preparation period, whether it be for the Back to Jerusalem movement or the next phase of God's journey for you and me, can leave us with more questions than answers. But as with the apostle Paul, the vision received was not a man-made one but a heavenly vision,[36] and nothing and no one could deflect him from being faithful to it. And so it must be for us, and God's vision for you and me to be a disciple and overcomer.

---

35. See Paul Hattaway, *Back to Jerusalem: Called to Complete the Great Commission* (Carlisle: Piquant Editions, 2003).
36. See Acts 26:19.

Back to Hezekiah

If you looked with the natural eye it would appear to be true that there is no way through tough, uncompromising times. Hezekiah could have just given in to the situation, believing that no change was possible. The truth of God's Word tells us something else. 'We walk by faith, not by sight' (2 Corinthians 5:7, RSV). We believe the promises of God – they are 'Yes' and 'Amen' in Jesus Christ (2 Corinthians 1:20). We believe in the character of God – he will never leave us or forsake us.[37] We obey the voice of God, no matter how foolish that may seem.

Hezekiah displayed the same attitude and belief as Mary when the angel told her, a virgin, that she would 'give birth to a son' (Luke 1:31). She replied, 'May it be to me as you have said' (Luke 1:38), believing what God has promised will come into being.

Preparing the way of the Lord[38] has a strong link to keeping safe that which he has given – experience, testimony and revelation of truth; it is protecting, making sure nothing and no one can steal from you;[39] it is guarding, 'Keep watch over yourselves and all the flock' (Acts 20:28), preserving, holding fast and nurturing all that God has shared.

Hezekiah had a necessary quality that would see revival come throughout the nation, and one that is essential for you and me today – a godly tenacity. Too many people have missed God's moment because they tried to go it alone in life and ministry. Too many people have missed God's moment because other treasure occupied their heart, causing them to let go and stop nurturing God's dream. Tenacity was replaced by indifference and duplicity. Not so with Hezekiah, but what about you and me?

---

37. See Hebrews 13:5.
38. See for example Isaiah 40:3.
39. See John 10:10.

Isaiah

We have already mentioned Isaiah's role in the life of Hezekiah. Isaiah was to understand that in the difficult, challenging and tough times God does not leave us to muddle through gallantly. God makes this very clear, but he does require us to be active.

> I will go before you and will level the mountains; I will break down gates of bronze and cut through bars of iron [to release prisoners]. I will give you the treasures of darkness, riches stored in secret places, so that you may know that I am the LORD, the God of Israel, who calls you by name.
>
> (Isaiah 45:2-3)

> Build up, build up, prepare the road! Remove the obstacles out of the way of my people.
>
> (Isaiah 57:14)

When God challenged his people to 'prepare the way for the LORD' (Isaiah 40:3) it was often at a crucial and difficult time. His aim was not to get us to put up the shutters and batten down the hatches with a 'grin and bear it' attitude. No! It was always a time to look up and not down, to get a fresh glimpse of God and his character, to understand what he longs to accomplish and do amongst his people, whatever the circumstances. And at the centre of this is the call to 'get ready to change'.

Remember what it means to prepare the way: To create a favourable environment or presence that makes it easy for the Spirit of God to enter into and operate sovereignly in the lives of people.

Remember God's promise: 'I am the LORD, your God, who takes hold of your right hand and says to you, Do not fear; I will help you' (Isaiah 41:13).

A conversation with the Lord

In the month of December a few years ago, I began to look ahead to the coming year, and particularly the ministry opportunities and accompanying travel plans. There is always a sense of anticipation, excitement, and also hesitation, as some of the challenges are far too daunting. The unexpected conversation with the Lord went like this.

God: I know what you have planned for this coming year: the places, opportunities, ministry openings. I want you to know, Mike, travelling to different parts of the world – the extreme heat of Bangkok and the cold of Mongolia, the incredible challenge of India and Nepal, eating strange food, struggling with jet lag – this *is the easy bit*! Also, teaching thirty hours a week, encouraging leaders, praying with people, speaking prophetic words over people's lives and grappling with the cultural divide *is the easy bit.*

Mike: OK, Lord. What is the difficult bit, then? If preaching, teaching, encouraging, sharing, giving, helping and bearing other's burdens is the easy bit, what is the difficult bit, Lord?

God: It is preparing the way for me in all of this. The activity of giving, sharing and ministry can be just a means of drawing attention to yourself. Doing things can leave the focus of attention on you. People don't need to be touched by your compassion, but by my love. People don't need to hear you speak, but me. People don't need to simply enjoy your company, but my Presence. The doing and serving can be 90 per cent about you and 10 per cent about me. It's time to reverse this percentage!

Mike: Lord, what does it mean to prepare the way for you? Please show me.

And he did:

'He [Jesus] must become greater; I must become less' (John 3:30).

How do we begin to 'make straight' the way of the Lord (Isaiah 40:3, KJV)? Perhaps these scriptures will give you a starting point:

1. Put your ego to one side – 'Do nothing out of selfish ambition' (Philippians 2:3).
2. Put the vision of what you want to do and how you want to do it to one side – do not 'look ... to your own interests' (Philippians 2:4). It is the ulterior motives we all have behind the spiritual veneer of our ministry that block God's path.
3. Don't make a platform for yourself to show how good and spiritual you are; just concentrate on humility and obedience.[40] God will exalt or 'lift you up in due time' (1 Peter 5:6).

If I do this, where will this lead me? I suspect to a place of mixed feelings. To a place of excitement about going down a new road with God, but also hesitation and uneasiness, realising the degree of personal challenge and change that will be need to be faced.

The central lesson I learned in all of this

Whatever blessing and experience I have received from God to date I sense will be insufficient for tomorrow's journey and ministry. I do not want to be yesterday's man in today's world. There is a desperate need for a new encounter with God to fill my emptiness. I must not be afraid

40. See Philippians 2:6-11.

of the unknown. I need to 'walk by faith' (2 Corinthians 5:7, RSV). It is time to look up, take courage and refocus. Be changed to the next degree God requires.

Prepare, be ready; there is much to receive and overcome. Understand that you have never been on this journey before – it is a new day. Understand that it is possible to be overfamiliar with life and ministry – do not operate on automatic pilot! Understand that there is a huge gap between where you are now spiritually and what God requires for the next stage of the journey – prepare the way of the Lord!

As we progress on this path of preparing and being ready, let's not forget what it means – it is worth repeating:

Remember what it means to prepare the way: To create a favourable environment or presence that makes it easy for the Spirit of God to enter into and operate sovereignly in the lives of people.

Some Questions

1. What encouragement and lessons can we learn from Hezekiah, Isaiah and our Chinese brothers and sisters?
2. Do you have someone able to speak into your life, to support, advise and prepare you for God's next move? How teachable are you?
3. If Jesus 'must become greater' and 'I must become less' (John 3:30), what needs to happen and change?

Chapter Eleven
The Importance of Revelation 1-3

In the last chapter we began by saying that Revelation is full of promises and warnings, and chapters 1-3 give us the starting point for this next phase of the journey: 'Prepare now for tomorrow!' … 'Get ready!' What we believe will happen in the future directly affects how we live in the present. The clear message coming through these early chapters is that to overcome the challenges of tomorrow and the future we need to be courageous and honest about our current life in the present. That is the clear message Jesus is communicating in these early chapters of Revelation. We will not be able to withstand external pressures and persecution if we have not dealt with the internal problems we have personally and in the Church now. So at a personal, ministry and church level, some straightforward and yet awkward questions need to be faced.

> What issues are we tempted to compromise on for the sake of relative peace, both in the Church and in society?
>
> How would Jesus speak into my life, ministry and church at this moment?
>
> If he was to say, 'Yet I hold this against you' (Revelation 2:4), what would follow?
>
> How real is the future hope in Christ? Does it shape the way we live today or not?

These are extremely penetrating questions, and the disciple desiring to become an overcomer will take them seriously. Getting ready and preparation has at its centre personal and corporate development, for we belong to the body of Christ. As we shall see in this chapter, our calling is in at least three areas: calling to character or personal holiness, calling to a relationship with God, and calling to service – a unique contribution in God's kingdom.

As we approach this chapter, it may be helpful to adopt a learning and discovery position. This can be through reflecting, asking yourself questions and then applying the learning. My desire is that the Spirit of God be your teacher and mine as we go deeper into understanding the challenge of becoming an overcomer. I trust that this will lead into new self-awareness, insight, ideas and learning attitudes. This in itself will take us into discovery and action and a deeper walk with God.

The promises of God to the seven churches

Let's focus briefly on the promises and the hope that is ours in Christ. In difficult and tough times the Holy Spirit shines or polishes the promise related to our future and hope. The Greek word for hope, *elpis*, has this definite assurance, come what may. To him (or her) who overcomes, what is the assured and certain prize?

> To him who overcomes, I will give the right to eat from the tree of life, which is in the paradise of God.
>
> (Revelation 2:7)

> To him who overcomes, I will give some of the hidden manna. I will also give him a white stone with a new name written on it, known only to him who receives it.
>
> (Revelation 2:17)

> To him who overcomes and does my will to the end, I will give authority over the nations …
>
> (Revelation 2:26)
>
> He who overcomes will, like them, be dressed in white. I will never blot out his name from the book of life, but will acknowledge his name before my Father and his angels.
>
> (Revelation 3:5)
>
> Him who overcomes I will make a pillar in the temple of my God. Never again will he leave it. I will write on him the name of my God and the name of the city of my God, the new Jerusalem, which is coming down out of heaven from my God; and I will also write on him my new name.
>
> (Revelation 3:12)
>
> To him who overcomes, I will give the right to sit with me on my throne, just as I overcame and sat down with my Father on his throne.
>
> (Revelation 3:21)

These promises are just too much for us to take in, and yet they are ours to embrace with everything that we own and have. However, they require us to re-evaluate our lives now, and to allow the Holy Spirit free access to make whatever changes to our lives he desires. It may be helpful at this point to remind ourselves that the author of Revelation is Jesus himself, and chapters 1-3 are spoken into the 'now' that I am writing this, and the 'now' that you are reading it. There is a current need to face both internal and external challenges. Three areas come immediately to mind for us individually and also as churches: compromise in belief and behaviour, tolerance of idolatry and tolerance of immorality.

The greatest tragedy is to throw away our eternal prospects because of temporary trouble. Above and beyond the challenge of temptation – and even suffering – that we may face are the towering promises that dwarf anything that the world may try to entice us away from.

Just give some time to think about the following: never to be hurt by the second death; personally invited to sit with Jesus on His throne; amazingly dressed in white garments; having a promised eternal place in the new heaven and new earth.

How glorious is that? Now we can perhaps see the truth that what we believe will happen in the future directly affects how we live in the present.

The church in *Ephesus* was applauded for its patience, persistence and discernment, the church in *Smyrna* for its courage and perseverance, the church in *Pergamum* for not denying the faith under pressure, the church in *Thyatira* for its love, patience and progress, and *Philadelphia* for its loyalty and support.

These churches had many excellent and praiseworthy qualities to their Christian lives as seen above, and we may be able to identify with them and say, 'That's me too. I think I'm doing pretty well, considering everything.' But while we are admiring our strengths, we must not let them cloud over and minimise our weaknesses. Hiding things from God has been a feature of fallen humanity right from Adam and Eve, and to continue to do so is to play into the hands of the devil and give him a foothold in our lives. Paul reminds us to be 'very careful' how we live (Ephesians 5:15), and not to 'give the devil a foothold' (Ephesians 4:27). After all, we are 'children of light' (Ephesians 5:8), not darkness. So to the same churches and to us, Jesus encourages us to be brave, and face up to our shortcomings and our more shadowy side. *Ephesus* had forsaken their first love. *Pergamum* and *Thyatira* were into idolatry and immorality. *Sardis* started new ventures but never finished anything. *Laodicea* was sick and didn't realise it; they prided themselves on warm fellowship but were lukewarm.

To the seven churches and to us Jesus does three things.

First, he encourages us to hear what the Spirit is saying, and then to heed and take action. Amid all the voices we are hearing in today's world, the Holy Spirit is speaking to do as Jesus said in John 14:26 – to 'teach [us] all things', and to 'remind [us] of everything [he has] said', and establish peace in troubled times and take away fear.

Secondly, he tells us to remember, repent and put things right, because faith is more than a feeling – it is something you do, it is obedience. Being led into all truth demands action and change, but it will lead to joy that no one can take way.

Thirdly, he tells us to hold on and not let go, whatever the challenge and level of opposition that may come our way. The major motivation for holding on is the confidence and assurance that Jesus will return and finally defeat all enemies, and establish his eternal kingdom, where we will enjoy new and complete bodies in a new and complete earth.

As I am writing this, I found myself asking this question, 'What quality is God challenging me to embrace?' For me, and maybe you too, I hear the Spirit speaking loudly: *courage*, be courageous! As we look through Scripture in the Old and New Testaments there are several aspects to courage that we need to be aware of.

Courage can fail (Joshua 2:11; 5:1; 2 Samuel 4:1; Psalm 107:26)

These verses show that the courage of unbelievers fails in the face of God's might and power, as with the kings of Jericho and the Amorites.

But it is also the courage of God's people Israel that fails in the face of uncertainty and peril. I don't need to labour the point, as I am all too aware of experiencing this at a personal level, and to my shame courage has failed all too often, and sometimes in only mildly challenging situations. It is through these times that the Spirit of God reminds us not to be complacent and overconfident, knowing that situations can influence us and cause our courage to melt.

Courage can be found, it can be taken hold of (2 Samuel 7:27; 2 Chronicles 15:8)

David found courage – how? It came by revelation, by God speaking and opening David's eyes to see the truth. Eyes and ears are so important in difficult and tough times. Where we look and whose voice we listen to will either lead us to defeat or to be overcomers.

Azariah spoke an anointed word to Asa: 'The Lord is with you when you are with him. If you seek him, he will be found by you, but if you forsake him, he will forsake you. ... But as for you, be strong and do not give up, for your work will be rewarded' (2 Chronicles 15:2,7). How did Asa respond? He took courage. He believed the spoken word by faith, and then acted on it by removing the idols, repairing the altar of the Lord, gathering all the people at Jerusalem, and sacrificing to the Lord, making a covenant to seek the Lord, the God of their fathers. Courage is far more than simply a feeling or attitude; it is always transferred into action and is visible, as seen in the following.

Courage is not an optional choice (Deuteronomy 31:6,7; Joshua 1:6-18; 1 Chronicles 28:20)

The Old Testament is peppered with examples of this. The formidable challenges faced by Joshua, Israel or David were opportunities, not to reassess whether they should have a change of mind and seek a more comfortable outcome, but to embrace the moment with courage, knowing that God was with them. His presence is sufficient in the face of any obstacle, challenge or level of opposition.

In the New Testament, in Acts 4:13 the priests, the captain of the temple guard, the Sadducees, the rulers, elders and teachers of the law and Caiaphas were formidable opponents to the message preached by Peter and John. Peter's preach from Acts 4:8-12 demonstrated one thing: that his courage did not come from himself but from the Holy Spirit. Peter's courage was *heard* as he refused to compromise the truth that salvation is found in no other name than Jesus Christ crucified, resurrected and ascended in glory. But Peter's courage was also *seen* – it was visible to all, and especially noted by his opponents. What conclusion did they draw from this? After all, the apostles were uneducated and ordinary men. Simply this: 'these men had been with Jesus' (Acts 4:13).

Courage is to be present and continuous

There is no indication that courage is a quality just for the occasional tough moment. The moment we believe is the beginning of seeing courage and confidence in our faith growing. It is a never-ending journey, and discovery is often filled with many ups and downs. There are moments when courage is suppressed and our faith wobbles, as the voices shouting out 'Compromise!' seem unconquerable. And yet there are other times, when we recover from these moments by humbling ourselves before God, and calling out like David in Psalm 51: 'Have mercy on me, O God' (v. 1), and 'Create in me a pure heart, O God, and renew a steadfast spirit within me. Do not cast me from your presence or take your Holy Spirit from me. Restore to me the joy of your salvation and grant me a willing spirit, to sustain me' (vv. 10-12). In these moments the Holy Spirit moves afresh in our lives, faith increases, truth is taken to a deeper level, and the vision of Christ on the throne in heaven, far above every principality and power, brings strength and courage for the next stage of the journey.

Let's finish off this chapter by listening to Paul encouraging and spurring on the church at Corinth and us. His rallying cry puts us on the front foot with an eagerness to continue the journey.

> Be on your guard; stand firm in the faith; be men of courage; be strong.
>
> (1 Corinthians 16:13)

At the beginning of this chapter I asked some questions. Look at them again in the light of what you have read.

Some Questions

1. What issues are we tempted to compromise on for the sake of relative peace, both in the Church and in society?
2. How would Jesus speak into my life, ministry and church at this moment? Evaluate your strengths and, in the light of Jesus' challenge to the seven churches, be honest in admitting weaknesses.
3. How do you move forward from question 2?
4. How real is the future hope in Christ? Does it shape the way we live today or not? Try to be practical in your assessment.

Chapter Twelve
Identifying Our Enemies and Dealing with Fear

> I keep asking that the God of our Lord Jesus Christ, the glorious Father, may give you the Spirit of wisdom and revelation, so that you may know him better. I pray also that the eyes of your heart may be enlightened in order that you may know the hope to which he has called you, the riches of his glorious inheritance in the saints, and his incomparably great power for us who believe. That power is like the working of his mighty strength, which he exerted in Christ when he raised him from the dead and seated him at his right hand in the heavenly realms, far above all rule and authority, power and dominion, and every title that can be given, not only in the present age but also in the one to come.
>
> (Ephesians 1:17-21)

Before we look at the very important issue of overcoming temptation and accusation, we need to see the supremacy of Christ and its importance to us now. This clear statement that Paul made to the church in Ephesus is the rock upon which we stand.

It is this last truth which must be the springboard for this chapter. In the book of Revelation, the throne of God moves to centre stage, and nowhere more so than in chapter 4. 'Throne' is the key word and refers to God's throne ten times and the throne of the twenty-four elders once. God reigns supreme above the battles of good and evil. He is worthy of our praise and worship. The truth to be received when the going gets tough is that God is on the throne and in control. He is working everything for good, and the message of Revelation gives us a message of hope to share in seasons of shaking. The invitation of the Spirit of God for John is the same for us today, namely, to come into the presence of God: 'Come up here, and I will show you' (Revelation 4:1). What will sustain us through trials, persecution, temptation and accusations? What will give us the strength and courage to hold on and fix our eyes on Jesus? Surely it is the truth that he sits on the throne, far above every power and authority, and that, as Paul says, his 'grace is sufficient for [me]', and his 'power is made perfect in weakness' (2 Corinthians 12:9). Paul adds to this in Romans 5:3 that, when sufferings come, we 'rejoice', knowing that the love of God poured into our hearts by the Holy Spirit will produce perseverance, character and hope, and 'hope does not disappoint' because Christ has overcome (v. 5).

We have three enemies

There are two important questions to ask. First, where does the spiritual opposition come from? Second, how do we overcome? To the first question Paul, Peter and John all help us understand this. The New Testament tells us about three enemies.

The world

In 2 Peter 1:4 he refers to the world as corrupt, and in this sense the world stands as a symbol of corruption. This world is hostile to God because its world view and lifestyle has no place for God and his kingdom. Paul makes the reason clear: because Satan is the 'god of this age' (2 Corinthians 4:4). If you love the world, you will embrace the value system that Satan promotes – the lust of the flesh, 'the lust of the eyes', and the boastful pride of life (1 John 2:16). This world is hostile to God's world, and will do everything in its power to entice and deceive us. John Calvin said, 'We may infer that the human mind is, so to speak, a perpetual forge of idols.'[41] We can make idols out of anything. Any passionate desire that is not put there by God and for his glory can become an idol. Loving the world is idolatry. Jesus' words both challenge us and comfort us in John 16:33: 'In this world you will have trouble. But take heart! I have overcome the world.'

The flesh

One meaning of flesh is simply normal human existence. Jesus became flesh and took on human form, becoming a man. But in our context being 'in the flesh' is to live and act sinfully.[42] Flesh refers to the rebellious human nature. Paul teaches that the fallen human nature is inherently rebellious against God. We inherited this nature from Adam, and unfortunately it was not eradicated when we became Christians. It is still within us, but we are no longer forced to follow its demands. As we see in Romans 8, we now have the Spirit within us, who is strong enough to keep the flesh from getting the upper hand. What kind of things does the flesh cause us to do? '... sexual immorality, impurity and debauchery; idolatry and witchcraft; hatred, discord, jealousy, fits of rage, selfish ambition, dissensions, factions and envy; drunkenness, orgies, and the like' (Galatians 5:19-21).

The flesh, our old self, and the Spirit are in conflict with each other, as we read in Galatians 5:17. 'What causes fights and quarrels among you? Don't they come from your desires that battle [*strateuō*] within you?' (James 4:1). If we feed the flesh, and give in to its desires, it will grow that much stronger. The flesh is the enemy of our soul or spirit, and wages war against it. The answer to the flesh, of course, is the power of the Spirit. Paul appeals to the will to start fighting, for the old self has been crucified with Christ, and we can walk in the newness of life.

41. John Calvin, *Institutes of the Christian Religion*, 1.11.8.
42. See Romans 8:4,5,7,12.

The devil, Satan

Peter makes this particularly clear: 'Your enemy the devil prowls around like a roaring lion looking for someone to devour' (1 Peter 5:8). Clearly, the devil is a real, personal being that opposes the Christian, and seeks to make them ineffective in their Christian life. He is a formidable enemy. Satan will use every tactic to blind people to the gospel.[43] He uses lies, deception, and every kind of destructive activity to cause people to turn away from God. Accusations and temptations are high on his list in order to cause doubt, guilt, fear, confusion, sickness, pride, slander, or any other means possible to hinder a Christian's witness and usefulness.

Dealing with fear

In difficult times, where are we looking for help? 'Let us fix our eyes on Jesus' (Hebrews 12:2). The writer was writing at a time of persecution; it was a tough time to be a Christian. Hebrews helps us understand that the moment we look at the problem or the enemy or the mountain of difficulties and take our eyes off Jesus then the following happens.

We begin to drift

Hebrews 2:1 instructs us to be careful so that 'we do not drift away'. Notice how clever Satan is! He puts us on a very subtle and slow path of turning away from God. At first you don't realise too much difference. Like an unsuspecting holidaymaker enjoying an afternoon relaxing on a floating sunbed in the shallows, and suddenly realising that the shore is a long way off, and they are now out of their depth and in danger.

We begin to doubt

As we drift, fear takes us to a new level, that of doubting. In Matthew

43. See 2 Corinthians 4:4.

14:30 Peter started to walk on water, but the more he looked at the wind and the waves the more fear gripped his heart, and he began to doubt and sink. However, the positive lesson from Peter is that in his fear he did the right thing. He cried out to Jesus, 'Lord, save me!'

We begin to deny

Fear will take us down this slippery slope unless we are very careful. We drift, then doubt, and end up denying. Peter again experienced this personally. After three years of following Jesus, he was one of the main disciples. However, when Jesus was arrested and about to be crucified, fear took hold of his heart. He had already promised that he would never forsake Jesus. Now, in the high priest's courtyard, he was challenged three times, and denied Jesus.[44] Fear took hold of him. Fear told him to save himself. Fear urged him to turn his back on Jesus.

'See to it that no-one takes you captive' (Colossians 2:8). This is exactly the intention of Satan, and in these last days he determines to make us fearful by any means, even a pandemic. The biggest fear most people have is the fear of death. We can list some other issues that fear would plant in our hearts.

> Fear leads us to forget the ways of God, and try to find a more comfortable alternative.
>
> Fear persuades us to break our relationship with God and go our own way.
>
> Fear convinces us that God can't do a miracle and set us free.
>
> Fear turns our eyes off God, and focus on the lifestyle of other people and nations.

44. See Mark 14:31,66-72.

Living with fear gradually becomes a lifestyle. Fear is not a healthy emotion for everyday life; it damages and destroys. We have seen this so clearly with the downturn in mental health as a result of the pandemic. Edward T. Welch said that 'worriers are visionaries minus the optimism'[45] – how true! But fear has its place, and through it, God intends to remove our self-reliance and come to our senses. Psalm 73 causes us to focus on what will carry us through fear and every struggle. When 'I entered the sanctuary of God; then I understood' (v. 17). 'My flesh and my heart may fail, but God is the strength of my heart and my portion for ever' (v. 26).

'Do not be afraid' is repeated time and time again in Scripture. They are words of comfort and reassurance, but they are also a command. Fear represents a choice that we make at a deep level. Who are we going to trust? We can't change the past. We don't know how the future will unfold. But we can change the way we think in the present. G.K. Chesterton once wrote that there are two sins against Christian hope: *the sin of presumption*, which assumes that everything will go well; no problems, struggles, testing and suffering; God taking us effortlessly through life and into his presence – and *the sin of despair*, which says that nothing and no one can help in the current situation; there is nothing to cling on to; we have been abandoned and we are on our own.[46] The challenge to not be afraid leads us to believe that the God of yesterday will be with us today and tomorrow. 'And surely, I am with you always, to the very end of the age' (Matthew 28:20).

Peter's practical advice

Peter in 1 Peter 3:14-15 tells us not to fear or be troubled. He also gives us understanding as to how we can come to that place in our spiritual

---

45. https//quotefancy.com/quote/2116202/Edward-T-Welch (accessed 22.6.22).
46. G.K. Chesterton, 'The History of a Half-Truth' in *Where All Roads Lead*, in *The Collected Works* (San Francisco, CA: Ignatius Press, 1991).

lives. We are living in a culture of fear – just read the newspapers and listen to the daily news. How then can I have hope in this culture of fear? It may be true to say that anything outside of our control produces fear. When we are on the throne of our lives the consequence of that will be fear, because we do not have full control over all that takes place in our lives. Peter's advice to dealing with fear in seen in verse 15: 'But in your hearts set apart Christ as Lord.'

The world, the flesh and Satan know that if we can be persuaded to take back the throne of our lives from Jesus, we will live in fear, with the possibility of drifting, doubting and denying. When Jesus is Lord of our lives then fear turns to confidence. Why? Because the sovereign Lord knew all about the circumstances of our birth, and he knows all about our life and death, yes, every single detail. He has walked through all that has happened in your past and all that will happen in your future, and all is under his perfect control. Psalm 139:16 says, 'All the days ordained for me were written in your book before one of them came to be.' Then fear is replaced by comfort and hope. In life and in death I am not my own but my body and soul belong to my faithful Saviour, Jesus Christ.

These words were written on the wall of a cellar in Germany at the end of the Second World War:

> I believe in the sun even when it is not shining
> And I believe in love, even when there's no one there.
> And I believe in God, even when He is silent.[47]

The removal of fear enables us to hear hope's melody of the future. The removal of fear enables us to dance to that melody in the present. 'Surely

47. Author unknown. See www.goodreads.com/quotes/9812347-i-believe-in-the-sun-even-when-it-is-not (accessed 8.6.22).

goodness and mercy will follow me all the days of my life' (Psalm 23:6). He is on my case, and he doesn't give up.

Some Questions

1. When did you last gaze with wonder and excitement of Jesus sitting on the throne in heaven? How can this help you?
2. What specific aspects of fear are currently challenging you?

Chapter Thirteen
Facing Accusations and Temptations Head-on

We have already referred to Satan as a lion roaring to scare, frighten and intimidate us. While some may have had this experience, others of us may have had a lesser sense of being frightened, scared and intimidated. But that is not his only line of attack. Paul tells us in 2 Corinthians 11:14 that he 'masquerades as an angel of light'. He is a master of deception and pretence. He will use false prophets, apostles, teachers and every kind of worker in order to bring a false sense of security, birthing complacency, self-satisfaction and false peace. We must remember the words of Jesus in John 10:10, 'The thief comes only to steal and kill and destroy', and he will use multiple ways to do this. To overcome it is necessary to face Satan's multiple tactics head-on.

There are two main activities of Satan highlighted in the Word of God, and no doubt we all will have had to face them. One is accusation, the other is temptation. Satan accuses with the sin that we have already done, and he tempts us to do the sin we have not yet done.

The Gospel writers in particular teach us that the Word of God abiding in us is the way we conquer the evil one in both these activities. Matthew, Mark and Luke show us that Jesus modelled this in his time of testing in the desert. The truth of God's Word stored up in the heart is a weapon to be used. It is referred to as a sharp two-edged instrument to defeat Satan's tactics in Hebrews 4:12. Jesus gives us a firm foundation for tackling temptations and accusations – the Word of God. His reply to the devil's cunning on all three occasions was, 'It is written' (Matthew 4:4), 'It is also written' (Matthew 4:7) and 'For it is written' (Matthew 4:10).

Before we look further into this, there is a question that may be helpful to be clarify. What is the difference between 'test' and 'tempt'?

Tests and trials

The New Testament teaching is clear: tests and trials are inevitable, a fact we have all experienced. It reminds us 'when' we face trials and not 'if' we face them. Satan will surely present us with tests and trials of every kind at every opportunity. But it is also true that God tests us through the daily challenges that come our way. What is the difference? Satan tests us through trials in the hope that we turn away from God, as with the disciples in John 6:66 who no longer followed Jesus. However, God allows tests and trials to strengthen and equip us. It is an opportunity for us to grow, mature, become stronger and bring increasing honour to God.

James 1:2-5,12 teaches us that testing is productive, not destructive. It 'develops perseverance', helps to mature us, and brings further completion to our spiritual lives. Amazingly, through this often uncomfortable and difficult time, the Holy Spirit brings a deeper level of joy than we have ever known before. How supernatural is that!

Trials may be hard to bear, but the reward, according to James 1:12, is astonishing: that we receive 'the crown of life'. The challenge is, do we look back to what was or look forward to what will be, and yes, the crown of life?

Satan in times of testing wants us to look back to the old life and make it appear so much better and more attractive than the present and the future. Remember the Israelites in the wilderness? They said that in Egypt they ate 'fish … cucumbers, melons, leeks, onions and garlic', but now they had nothing to eat but manna (Numbers 11:5-6). However, God in times of testing wants us to look forward, and that surely is central to the book of Revelation. How tragic to be like Esau, who gave up his inheritance for a bowl of soup![48] Through the whole

48. See Hebrews 12:16.

book of Revelation the Holy Spirit is calling us to hold on, be steadfast, be faithful to the end, so that like Job we will 'come forth as gold' (Job 23:10).

> … we also rejoice in our sufferings, because we know that suffering produces perseverance; perseverance, character; and character, hope. And hope does not disappoint us, because God has poured out his love into our hearts by the Holy Spirit, whom he has given us.
>
> (Romans 5:3-5)

Temptations

James 1:13-15 explains carefully that temptation does not originate with God, for he is holy. The cause of temptation is two-fold – Satan himself[49] and our flesh. Temptation entices us to disobey God and gratify our fleshly desires. Yielding or giving in to these desires puts us on a destructive path – it gives birth to sin, and sin, when it is given room and opportunity to grow, 'gives birth to death' (James 1:14-15).

Temptation therefore has its origin in Satan. His very nature is to tempt, and we can see this throughout the Scriptures. Here are just a few examples.

In the garden of Eden, Satan was disguised as a serpent to tempt Eve. To disobey God seems so much more attractive and beneficial than obeying. In Exodus, when Moses was up the mountain with God and he had been away so long, and not knowing when he would return, it seemed sensible to those left behind to seek alternative help and to make the golden calf to lead them. In Numbers 14, on finding out that Canaan

49. See 1 Peter 5:8.

was flowing with milk, honey and fruit, the size of the opposition caused the Israelites to look back to Egypt. In the book of Job, Satan tried to tempt Job to curse God, and he used every means available, even Job's wife.

In the New Testament nothing has changed. In Matthew 4, Satan attempts to tempt Jesus to act independently from his Father and the Holy Spirit. In Matthew 17, Peter, James and John witness something that is beyond words: Jesus has been transfigured before their eyes into a radiant appearance as the Son of God in heaven. He stood before them talking to two of the greatest heroes of Israel: Moses and Elijah. Peter's mistake, and the temptation of many through the ages, is to make Jesus equal to Moses and Elijah. The voice of God the Father from heaven both rebuked and corrected Peter's error. In Luke 22:31, Satan desired to have Peter and 'sift [him] as wheat'. He knows and exploits our weaknesses, and Peter that very day denied Jesus three times. Satan works within churches to tempt and to turn members away from God and from each other. The pandemic meant we were not able to meet together as church, except on a few occasions. Even though restrictions have now been lifted, the temptation to continue to be isolated from one another is very real.

Truth is under attack

When facing either temptations or accusations, the centre of attack is the mind, and truth is the target. There is a battle raging between the spirit of the age and the Word of Truth. What are some current challenges? Paul wrote in 1 Timothy 4:16, 'Watch your life and doctrine closely.' It may be helpful at this point to share briefly along these lines.

At this critical moment we would do well to weave the attitude of the Berean believers into our desire to be an overcomer. In Acts 17:11

we read that they 'examined the Scriptures' daily. It has been said that attitude determines our altitude, and the Bereans' dedicated attitude to understanding and applying the Word of God to their daily lives determined the closeness and intimacy with the presence of God.

When Paul mentions doctrine, it is not intended to be theoretical, boring and an academic pastime for a few intellectuals in a classroom. It is meant to be relevant and practical to all, resulting in praise to God. Paul's emphasis and ministry pattern is very focused. In his teaching to the Galatians, Ephesians, Philippians, Colossians and 1 Thessalonians, the doctrinal message comes first. Upon that foundation he builds the practical application, making the logical connection between the word and a practical application in life. Why? So that Christ, who loved the Church and gave his life for her, may present us to himself in splendour, 'without stain or wrinkle' (Ephesians 5:25-27).

Doctrine is what the whole Bible teaches us today about particular topics. Paul understood that having a firm foundation of truth in your life puts you in a great position to stand, and having 'done everything, to stand' (Ephesians 6:13). It helps us overcome our wrong ideas and the cultural pressure to tone down our fervour for Christ. It enables us to be able to make better decisions on current topical challenges. There are a few that immediately come to mind.

New Age thinking places the emphasis on freedom and authority for you to do and act as you like. 'If something feels good it must be OK.' Truth is not important, experience is!

Gender flexibility is a delicate and complex issue. Some believe that gender flexibility in our culture will increase our overall well-being.

Marriage of a man to a woman is no longer the only choice. There are many acceptable options: not to marry but just live together as husband and wife; choose to live with another man or another woman in same-sex commitment.

Multi-faith – all religions are good, and we must therefore live in harmony and acceptance of others' choice of faith. It is not right to try to change someone's beliefs.

Nominal belief or faith is normal. You can believe in Jesus and still organise, run and choose the kind of life you want to live. In other words, receive Jesus as Saviour but reject him as Lord!

Beware of an overemphasis on love at the expense of truth

Our culture today force-feeds us a false notion of love. The Beatles' song 'All You Need is Love' expressed that idea. Tolerance and diversity are its defining features. Meanwhile, in our current culture, absolute truth is generally held in high suspicion – if not treated with outright contempt. An unyielding commitment to 'truth' is often viewed as unloving. As a result, there is the danger that truth is sacrificed in the name of love.

Love and truth complete one another. The symbiotic relationship between love and truth is essential. Authentic love 'rejoices with the truth' (1 Corinthians 13:6). Love without truth has no character. Truth without love has no power. Love deprived of truth deteriorates into self-love. Truth divorced from love breeds self-righteousness. Jesus is our example, combining love and truth perfectly.

Love and *truth* are key words in John's second letter. The central theme throughout is the interdependence of these two qualities of Christ-likeness. John never lost his zeal for the truth, but he connected it to Christ-like love. We must walk in truth by displaying love (vv. 1-5). Truth is the foundation of love (vv. 1-3). Love is the fulfilment of truth (vv. 4-5). We must walk in love by devoting ourselves to truth (vv. 6-13). We must know the truth (vv. 6-9). We must guard the truth (vv. 10-12).

Paul's passion for doctrinal truth and John's testimony and teaching prepare us to face temptation, but also as we face accusations and lies.

Accusations and lies

Accusations together with temptation are two of the greatest activities of Satan. The very name Satan means accuser or adversary.

> Now have come the salvation and the power and the kingdom of our God, and the authority of his Christ. For the accuser of our brothers, who accuses them before our God day and night, has been hurled down. They overcame him by the blood of the Lamb and by the word of their testimony; they did not love their lives so much as to shrink from death.
>
> Revelation 12:10-11

John means that Satan's accusations do not have to be successful in harming and destroying our lives. They can be conquered when believers trust in the blood of the Lamb, Jesus Christ, to cover all their sins, and make that truth their testimony, even if it costs them their lives. They may die from persecution, but they are more than conquerors over the accuser. The accusations of Satan are nullified when we are under the blood of the Lamb – that is, when we are trusting in, walking with and united with the Son of God who died for us. In other words, this is effective to all who are connected to Jesus' death as their death, and his righteousness counts as their righteousness.

> My dear children, I write this to you so that you will not sin. But if anybody does sin, we have one who speaks to the Father in our defence – Jesus Christ, the Righteous One. He is the atoning

> sacrifice for our sins, and not only for ours, but also for the sins of the whole world.
>
> 1 John 2:1-2

The aim of John's letter is two-fold: that we do not sin, and that if we do sin, Satan is not able to accuse us in such a way that we despair of holiness and heaven, and just walk away into empty worldliness.

Key factors in overcoming accusations and lies

Jesus is the propitiator and advocate, meaning that he has satisfied the wrath of God and its demand for punishment. He bore 'the curse' for us (Galatians 3:13), so that the removal of God's wrath is secured. Because of this, Christ today is our advocate in heaven before God. In other words, if any accusation comes against us, Christ presents to God the infinite worth of his own blood and righteousness to cover all our sins, and successfully pleads our case – read Romans 8:33. John continues in 1 John 3:8 that this is the 'reason the Son of God appeared', to nullify and destroy the works of the devil.

> I write to you, young men, because you are strong, and the word of God lives in you, and you have overcome the evil one.
>
> (1 John 2:14b)

The heart of Satan's work, played out in a thousand ways, is to convince us that God is bad and sin is better. God's Word liberates us and gives us strength, saturating our minds with truth. Truth about Christ, truth about the cross, truth about the resurrection, and truth about the Holy Spirit enables us to 'Fight the good fight of the faith' (1 Timothy 6:12).

Colossians 3:16 tells us, 'Let the word of Christ dwell in you richly' – that is, abundantly, taking root in every corner of our lives, enabling us to combat every tactic that Satan may throw at us.

What picture comes to mind when you think of an overcomer? Some amazing spiritual Goliath? Some brilliant academic mind? Some practical planner and thinker? Someone with limitless energy? If that was the case, most of us would be excluded.

Let's remind ourselves of some important truths. God does not need our strengths but our weaknesses. When we run out of answers and our confidence and strength are at an all-time low, then, with nowhere else to turn but to God, we are in a position to be most effective. No one is too weak to experience God's power, but often we are too confident in our own ability and strength to receive it.

> You, dear children, are from God and have overcome them, because the one who is in you is greater than the one who is in the world.
>
> (1 John 4:4)

A brief summary of God's pathway in temptation and testing and accusations

Do not be surprised when these come. Be ready, clothed with the armour of God, making sure that the 'shield of faith' and the 'helmet of salvation' are firmly in place (Ephesians 6:16-17). Store up the Word of Truth in your heart. Satan's tactic is for you to doubt God's Word. The most dangerous point, and the place where the battle rages the strongest, is when God begins to anoint you and use you. 'You are now capable.' 'God has given you a great testimony, you are really somebody special.' 'You can go it alone. You don't need anyone's help from here on.' Beware!

The truth is that we are not as spiritual as we think we are! Be humble and submit yourself to God.[50] Only God can handle the devil, and he can only handle him through us if we are living in submission, obedience and dependence.

On final and important question as we finish this chapter.

What if we fail and fall?

There are some key verses that have really helped me.

> Do not gloat [rejoice] over me, my enemy! Though I have fallen, I will rise. Though I sit in darkness, the LORD will be my light.
>
> (Micah 7:8)

> My dear children, I write this to you so that you will not sin. But if anybody does sin, we have one who speaks to the Father in our defence – Jesus Christ, the Righteous One. He is the atoning sacrifice for our sins, and not only for ours but also for the sins of the world.
>
> (1 John 2:1-2)

Someone has redefined success like this: 'Success is not simply doing what is right, but it is our response to failure.'[51] Why? Because we all fail and make mistakes. *The key issue is the way we think at this point of failure!* Paul says in 1 Corinthians 2:16 that we have been given 'the mind of Christ', that is, the ability in every situation, no matter how

50. See James 4:7.
51. See e.g. Amy C. Edmondson, 'Strategies for Learning from Failure', *Harvard Business Review*, April 2011.

tough, to come through in victory. 2 Corinthians 2:14 says that God always leads us into victory.

The critical issue is, will we learn from our mistakes and use our failure to grow, mature, and be changed to be more like Jesus, or not? At this point we have two options:

1. To miss the opportunity to grow. How?

By refusing to take responsibility for our mistakes. By trying to cover up the mistake and pretend it didn't happen. This begins a trail of lies, deceiving people, hurting others and more particularly, damaging ourselves. By blaming others: 'After all, it really wasn't my fault. I have been working too hard, you don't understand the pressure I have been under. Others are more responsible for my mistakes than myself.' When we find ourselves reacting like this, we repeat the same mistakes over and over again, and this becomes a lifestyle. We begin to live the lie, and because we have failed, we believe that there is no way forward and no hope. The personal conclusion is falsely made, 'I am a failure!'

2. To grasp the opportunity to develop and change

Remember, success is not simply doing what is right, but is our response to failure. Why? Because we all fail and make mistakes. The key issue is the way we think at this point of failure! Remember what Paul says in 2 Corinthians. 2:14: 'God leads us in triumphal procession in Christ'. Success can come out of failure.

Perhaps David's response to failure in Psalm 51 may help us and show us the pathway to take at this critical moment. He calls on the mercy of God, and his 'unfailing love'. He receives the cleansing and forgiveness of God. He shows a genuine and renewed desire to live by truth, and to be taught God's wisdom. He believes that his life can be filled with joy and gladness in the presence of God. His crowning declaration is an inner cry for a pure heart and a contrite spirit – that without doubt is failure turned into success!

Some Questions

1. Summarise what has been important for you as we have looked at temptations and accusations.
2. Do you have the same appetite as the Bereans with regard to Scripture? How important to you are the Scriptures? Review your personal and family times (if appropriate) of reading God's Word.
3. To 'be able to stand your ground, and after you have done everything, to stand' (Ephesians 6:13) – what doctrinal truths do you need to review, rejoice in, and take to heart?

Section Three: Crucial Knowledge and Understanding to Overcome

Chapter Fourteen
Assurance and Confidence in the Promises of God

We are beginning to see that an overcomer, like the rainbow, is not a singular colour or attribute, but a mixture of many. It includes understanding our enemies, dealing with fear, overcoming accusations and temptations, tests and trials. Two qualities stand out to me at this juncture – assurance and confidence. Paul is a tremendous encouragement at this point.

> Therefore we do not lose heart. Though outwardly we are wasting away, yet inwardly we are being renewed day by day. For our light and momentary troubles are achieving for us an eternal glory that far outweighs them all.
>
> (2 Corinthians 4:16-17)

Paul explains the setting of this amazing truth. The god of this world had not blinded his eyes.[52] They had been opened by the truth of God's Word and the ministry of the Holy Spirit. He can now shine in a dark world. He can reflect the knowledge and 'the glory of God in the face of Christ' (2 Corinthians 4:6), no matter what the situation or challenge.

What does Paul call 'light and momentary troubles'? It is being 'hard pressed on every side, but not crushed; perplexed, but not in despair; persecuted, but not abandoned; struck down, but not destroyed' (2 Corinthians 4:8-9).

2 Corinthians 11:23-29 amplifies this for us: in prison frequently; flogged severely; 'exposed to death again and again'; five times receiving

52. See 2 Corinthians 4:4.

'forty lashes minus one'; three times 'beaten with rods'; once stoned; three times shipwrecked; 'in danger from rivers ... bandits ... [his] own countrymen [and]... Gentiles', in cities, towns and at sea; often going hungry, without food and drink.

How does Paul cope with what he calls – astonishingly – his 'light and momentary troubles'? To the natural mind it makes no sense. When the lights go out and we are confronted with the most unlikely challenges in front of us, our fleshly senses scream at us, 'Let go, get out, beat a hasty retreat and save yourself!' But to the mind renewed by the Spirit we are led to a remarkable insight that is the foundation of becoming an overcomer. The true gift of the Spirit is not only to give life, but to lead us into all truth. I make no apologies for repeating this. In John 6:68 Peter exclaims, 'Lord, to whom shall we go? You have the words of eternal life.' It is truth that sets us free.[53] It is truth that lifts our natural eyes to see beyond the troubles and hardships to where Christ is, sitting above all in glory. In these tough, uncompromising times the call of Revelation 4:1 sounds like a trumpet: 'Come up here'. See who is sitting on his throne, and listen to the angels singing, 'You are worthy, our Lord and God, to receive glory and honour and power' (v. 11). When this happens, that glimpse of Christ in glory, and our eternal future with him, may be the only reason why Paul would call his sufferings 'light and momentary'. The heroes of faith in Hebrews 11 must have seen the same, and it became their strength in remaining faithful even in death.

The foundation of confidence is knowledge and understanding sown into our hearts by the Spirit. They are vital in overcoming, and Paul and John would speak to our hearts today. True faith is made stronger by truth. Truth revealed by the Spirit enables us to trust more and more, especially when facing 'light and momentary troubles'.

---

53. See John 8:32.

Confidence and assurance combine faith, trust and belief in the truth of God's Word, the finished work of Christ, and his amazing promises that are complete in him.[54] These cover the whole span of our lives, past, present and future. Truth renewing our minds is transferred into strength and courage to act.

> That is why I am suffering as I am. Yet I am not ashamed, because I know whom I have believed, and am convinced that he is able to guard what I have entrusted to him for that day.
>
> (2 Timothy 1:12)

Graham Staines

Graham Staines had been working in Odisha, India since 1965 at the Mayurbhanj Leprosy Home, an evangelical missionary organisation caring for people who had leprosy, and looking after the tribal people in the area who lived in abject poverty. He took over the management of the Mission at Baripada in 1983. He also played a role in the establishment of the Mayurbhanj Leprosy Home as a registered society in 1982. He met Gladys in June 1981 while working for leprosy patients, and they married in 1983. They had three children: Esther, Philip and Timothy. In addition, Graham assisted in translating a part of the Bible into the Ho language of India, including proofreading the entire New Testament manuscript, though his focus was on a ministry to leprosy patients. He spoke fluent Oriya, and was very popular among the patients, whom he used to help after they were cured. He used to teach them how to make mats out of rope, and baskets from sabai grass and trees' leaves.

Wilma and I, together with our children, Paul, Esther and Karen, first met Graham, Gladys and family at Hebron School in South India. We

54. See 2 Corinthians 1:20.

enjoyed many half-term breaks together in the Nilgiri Hills of South India. Hebron School is still today an amazing gift for missionaries working in India and South East Asia, offering superb education in a Christian environment. We had all been together just weeks before Graham and his two sons Philip (aged ten) and Timothy (aged six) were burned to death in India by members of a Hindu fundamentalist group named Bajrang Dal.

On the night of 22 January 1999, Graham had attended a jungle camp in Manoharpur, an annual gathering of Christians of the area. The village is on the border of the tribal-dominated Mayurbhanj and Keonjhar districts of Orissa. He was on his way to Keonjhar with his sons, who had come back on holiday from their school at Ooty. They broke the journey for the camp, and spent the night in Manoharpur, sleeping in the vehicle because of the severe cold. Gladys had stayed back in Baripada. According to reports, a mob of about fifty people, armed with axes and other implements, attacked the vehicle while Graham and the children were fast asleep. Graham, Philip and Timothy were burned alive. Some villagers tried to rescue them, but were unsuccessful. Graham and the boys tried to escape, but the mob allegedly prevented their attempt.

Gladys continued to live and work in India, and we continued to meet her and Esther in Hebron. Gladys carried on caring for those who were poor and affected by leprosy, until she returned home to her native country of Australia in 2004. In 2005 she was awarded the fourth highest honour a civilian can receive in India, the Padma Shree, in recognition of her work in Odisha. In 2016 she received the Mother Teresa Memorial International Award for Social Justice.

For the apostles and men of God like Graham and women like Gladys, such was the reality of their relationship with God that it translated into a boldness, confidence and joy in dedicated serving, knowing that 'to live is Christ and to die', even as a martyr, 'is gain' (Philippians 1:21).

Confidence must embrace continuance

This is the central truth running through all these chapters. Our testimony does not simply point to a past event, but to a current reality. It continues day by day until our last breath. Below are a few verses that have meant so much to me.

While imprisoned in Rome and under house arrest, Paul writes to the Philippian church. Christianity was still young. Greed, sinfulness and sexual promiscuity were rampant throughout the Roman Empire. Paul's heart was to lead by example, and encourage the believers to press on, to take hold of everything that Christ gives, believing that he gives strength for every task and challenge.

> being confident of this, that he who began a good work in you will carry it on to completion until the day of Christ [the consummation of all things] …
>
> (Philippians 1:6)

For Paul, the gospel is not just a message heard yesterday, but one that needs to be held on to with tenacity and courage today. In Colossians 1:23 he emphasises this, and you can feel his pastoral heart of concern that some may turn back.

> if you continue in your faith, established and firm, not moved from the hope held out in the gospel. This is the gospel that you heard …

In Hebrew 3:14,15 the writer is communicating at a time of great testing. He urges believers to remember all that is shared in Christ, and to safeguard this at all costs.

> … if we hold firmly till the end the confidence we had at first. As has just been said: 'Today, if you hear his voice, do not harden your hearts as you did in the rebellion.'

In the book of Hebrews this determined confidence and hope in God is likened to an anchor. The anchor became a key Christian symbol during the period of Roman persecution. The first-century symbol of Christianity wasn't just the cross; it was also an anchor. To a first-century Christian hiding in the catacombs in Rome, and aware that many friends had just been martyred, by being either thrown to the lions or set ablaze as torches at one of Emperor Nero's garden parties, the symbol that would have encouraged them the most in their faith was an anchor. Epitaphs on believers' tombs dating as far back as the end of the first century frequently displayed anchors alongside messages of hope.

> We have this hope as an anchor for the soul, firm and secure.
>
> (Hebrews 6:19)

While this is a tremendous source of encouragement, the Holy Spirit brings a timely challenge, so that confidence is not replaced by complacency.

> So do not throw away your confidence; it will be richly rewarded. You need to persevere so that when you have done the will of God, you will receive what he has promised.
>
> (Hebrews 10:35-36)

The important question needs to be asked. What could cause you and me to throw away our confidence?

Hebrews was written to believers who had suffered much for their faith in Jesus. They had endured hardships, but still remained faithful to the call of God, and to their firm belief in God's salvation and promises. Having believed that God would turn their tragedies into victories, could it be that the longer the struggles, difficulties, hostility and persecution continue, the more those termite-like doubts begin to creep in? Hebrews 2:1 tells us to be careful not to 'drift away'. This becomes a slippery slope that can lead to a hardening of heart,[55] doubting and finally denial.

The Greek word translated 'throw away' is taken from the word *apoballo*. This is a compound of the words *apo* meaning 'away' and *ballo* meaning 'to throw something'. Therefore it means to throw away, to discard or to get rid of something no longer desired, needed or wanted.

Being aware of this challenge, I began to write down what could cause me to throw away my faith and trust. I initially thought of *weariness*[56] from running the race, serving others, and from the spiritual battle. Then I reflected again on areas already mentioned in this book: failure, and falling prey to accusations and temptations. But the Holy Spirit brought to my attention another topic that I have so often overlooked: *impatience.*

Living in today's world, impatience seems just a normal and everyday response to the unexpected and unwanted things that daily cross our paths. Spiritually, impatience, especially towards the promises of God, can cause us to respond to the unexpected and unwanted in a variety of ways. When impatience is given the opportunity to roam freely in my life, the result can be catastrophic. It can cause me to turn my eyes away from God, to act prematurely and unwisely, causing me to doubt the wisdom of waiting for God in trust and dependence upon him. Impatience unloosed can have a corrupting influence upon me, in the

55. See Hebrews 3:8,15; 4:7.
56. See Galatians 6:9.

same way that it did in Exodus 32, when in Moses' absence the people built a golden calf.

Will God ever turn my mourning into dancing? Is He really going to turn my ashes into beauty?[57] How much longer must I wait for the promise of God to come to pass? After all, the Church seems to be shrinking numerically, people are going out of the back door faster than entering the front. If I hadn't stood firmly on the Word of God all these years, at least I could have done something else with my life! Let's just forget the promises of God, and do something different, and rejoin the modern world.

In Hebrews 10:35 we see God's response, and the cry of his heart to ours is, hold tight and never let go of the promises he has made. The word 'confidence' in the Greek language is *parrhessia*. It means boldness, and depicts a very bold, frank and outspoken kind of language. It carries the meaning of being forthright, blunt, direct and straight to the point. Be bold and strong; be fearless in both declaring your faith and holding fast to the promises of God. Hebrews 10:35 could be rendered: 'Don't discard, dispel, dismiss, dump or cast off your bold declaration of faith, because it can have great reward.'

Some Questions

1. Reflect on assurance and confidence; what would cause you to drift and doubt?
2. Most of us at times will face disappointment. How do you come through this with your anchor still in place?
3. When God gives you a promise, what do you do next? How do you move forward?

57. See Isaiah 61:3.

Chapter Fifteen
The Death and Resurrection of Jesus Changed Everything

The death and resurrection of Jesus take me back to the end of the Gospels, and the beginning of God's New Day in Acts. What I see in the life of the disciples, and also the gathering of 120 in Acts 1, fills my heart to overflowing with thanksgiving and praise at the mercy and grace of God. It was an unexpected discovery that failure is now not final. What a relief to the disciples and also to us!

Acts has inspired many of us at an individual and corporate level and continues to do so today. To follow the sequence of events from uncertainty and fear in Acts 1 to a place of remarkable discovery, spiritual experience and anointing of the Spirit in Acts 2 is breathtaking. The exploits of a dedicated gathering of 3,120 at the end of Acts 2 and the subsequent numerical growth and geographical advance as we follow the early Church on its mission is remarkable. It focused on their desire to be faithful to the Great Commission in Matthew 28:18-20 and Acts 1:8… to 'make disciples of all nations'. As the power of the Holy Spirit came upon them, they will be able to be Christ's witnesses in Jerusalem, Judea, Samaria 'and to the ends of the earth'.

Yes, they were filled with the joy of knowing God even praising him in prison. Yes, they feared God. Yes, they were full of hope and courage, not obeying Jewish leaders but supremely God. Yes, they were prepared to lay down their lives. Yes, there was spontaneous evangelism as the Spirit empowered them. Yes, they were fearless in declaring the gospel in the face of opposition. But there is something much more wonderful to celebrate.

The apostolic teaching in the New Testament prevents us from exalting the exploits of human beings and being guilty, like the people of Lystra, of declaring that Paul and Barnabas were gods 'in human form' (Acts 14:11). One of Jesus' most damning criticisms of the Pharisee leaders is that 'they loved praise from men more than praise from God' (John 12:43). Paul was only too aware that his ability to be the missionary he was, and to have the success he did, was not founded on his human strength, ability and know-how. Every ounce of his ability to overcome and triumph over every one of the hardships and challenges we have mentioned has its root in two central truths: the cross and the resurrection of Jesus.

The cross

Paul makes his position very clear in Galatians 6:14: 'May I never boast except in the cross of our Lord Jesus Christ, through which the world has been crucified in me, and I to the world.' 'Boast' carries the meaning of rejoicing and glorying in something. What glory is there in the cross? It was an instrument of torture and shame. Why did Paul glory in it? He gloried in it because the most selfless act ever performed by anyone took place upon it. He saw – emanating from that rough beam upon which the Son of God had been crucified – the radiant hope of the world, the end of the believer's bondage to sin, which becomes real as the love of God is poured into our lives. To comprehend the mystery of Christ's atonement is impossible without the Holy Spirit illuminating truth to our hearts. I only know that all who come to the cross in simple, trusting faith can know and experience the loss of all their guilt and sin, and find peace with God. What a gift! 'Therefore, since we have been justified through faith, we have peace with God through our Lord Jesus Christ' (Romans 5:1).

The person at peace with God is a person whose mind is at rest about their relationship with God. One who knows God loves them despite their sin, they simply look to the cross and see Jesus.[58] They are now able to answer their conscience when accusations arise, trying to rake up the past. They no longer fear death and judgement.[59] When a person who knows the peace of God is suddenly overtaken by sin, they do not collapse and say, 'I've lost everything now!', but know instead that we have an advocate, one who 'speaks … in our defence' to the Father, Jesus Christ (1 John 2:1). Peace ushers us into the presence of God. and we are acceptable to God.

John in his first letter writes these words at the beginning of the third chapter: 'How great is the love the Father has lavished on us … !' This can be linked with John 3:16, 'For God so loved the world that he gave his one and only Son ...' I will briefly mention just three explanations of this lavish love.

First, it shows and demonstrates how much God loves us, even when we do not acknowledge or respond in any way to his love.[60] He desires a relationship with us as a child in his family. This is both now in this life and eternally, hence 'but have eternal life' (John 3:16).

Second, the cross demonstrates his justice. God, being righteous and just, had to find a way that the penalty due to us because of our sin could be fully paid. Speaking of God, Moses says, '… all his ways are just. A faithful God who does no wrong, upright and just is he' (Deuteronomy 32:4). If God did not punish sin he would be seen to act against his character, and act in an unrighteous way. Paul teaches in Romans 3:25-26 that when God sent Christ (the just and righteous one) as a sacrifice for our sin (the unjust and unrighteous ones) it demonstrated

58. See Romans 5:6-11.
59. See Hebrews 2:14-15
60. See Ephesians 2:1-5.

his righteousness. The punishment of sin has now been fully paid. He now justifies the person who has faith in Jesus his Son. The cross proves that God is just.

Third, to destroy the works of evil. 'The reason the Son of God appeared was to destroy the devil's work' (1 John 3:8). What happened on the cross broke the power of sin, death and hell. It dealt with our past, rescuing us out of the kingdom of darkness 'into the kingdom of the Son he loves' (Colossians 1:13). And Paul continues in Colossians that this love 'disarmed the powers and authorities' against us, 'triumphing over them by the cross' (Colossians 2:15). It deals with our past, present and future.

In Colossians 1:21-23 Paul speaks of this incredible journey from being alienated from God and classed as his enemy to being reconciled to God through the death of Christ. But the journey must continue: 'if you continue in your faith, established and firm, not moved from the hope held out in the gospel. This is the gospel that you heard and that has been proclaimed to every creature under heaven, and of which I, Paul, have become a servant' (v. 23). God's favour towards us is expressed very intimately and beautifully in Psalm 85:10, 'Love and faithfulness meet together; righteousness and peace kiss each other.' The Lord gives us what is good, and there is nothing better than peace with God through the cross.

The resurrection

Paul in 1 Corinthians 15 reminds his readers of the essence of the gospel. Our salvation is secure if we hold firmly to the following: 'Christ died for our sins ... was buried' – but it doesn't finish there – and 'was raised on the third day.' He continues that if Christ was not resurrected, then our faith is 'in vain' (KJV)! The resurrection of Jesus radically transformed the lives of the disciples, as the ascended and glorified Jesus of Nazareth poured out the Holy Spirit on the 120 at Pentecost (Acts 2:32-34).

The resurrection of Jesus declares once and for all that the power of God has triumphed over every aspect of darkness, past, present and future. *No wonder* that in Acts 2 the lives of the 120 were totally transformed. *No wonder* that people came running, asking questions, seeing and hearing truth for the first time, with the result that 3,000 believed, were baptised, and received the Holy Spirit. *No wonder* that the religious authorities were confused (Acts 4), seeing a crippled beggar healed (Acts 3), and that 'unschooled, ordinary men' (v. 13) were demonstrating what Jesus did and what he taught. There was only one explanation: 'these men had been with Jesus' (v. 13). *No wonder* the Church grew and multiplied in Jerusalem, Judea, Samaria, Asia Minor, Europe and Rome, and yes, to 'the ends of the earth' (Acts 1:8). *No wonder* the opposition grew, and persecution became the norm in the early Church.

Stephen was the first martyr of many. *They bear witness* to the truth and reality of knowing that there is salvation in no name other than Jesus Christ.[61] *They bear witness* to the truth and reality of knowing that they belong to the kingdom of God and the Age to Come. *They bear witness* to the truth and reality that nothing can separate us from the love of God in Jesus,[62] and nothing could tempt them away from holding on to the very end and that last breath. ('Truth' and 'reality' are the same words in Hebrew and Greek.)

61. See Acts 4:11.

62. See Romans 8:38-39.

The significance of the resurrection

It ensures our new birth

> … he has given us new birth into a living hope through the resurrection of Jesus Christ from the dead …
>
> (1 Peter 1:3)

Our life now is resurrection life. We have not received all of our resurrection life, because our bodies remain subject to weakness, ageing and death. But our spirits have been made alive with new resurrection power. That is why Paul can say, 'made us alive with Christ' and 'raised us up' together with him (Ephesians 2:5-6; Colossians 3:1). Paul connects the resurrection of Christ with the spiritual power at work within us.

> … his incomparably great power for us who believe. That power is like the working of his mighty strength, which he exerted in Christ when he raised him from the dead and seated him at his right hand in the heavenly realms. (Ephesians 1:19-20)

This new resurrection power in us includes power to gain more and more victory over the remaining sin in our lives, but also provides power for ministry in the work of the kingdom.

It ensures our justification

> He was delivered over to death for our sins and was raised to life for our justification.
>
> (Romans 4:25)

The resurrection was God's approval of Christ's redemptive work. It demonstrated that there was no penalty for sin left to pay, and the victory over death declares that our sins have been forgiven, and we are seen as righteous in God's sight. To condemn is to declare someone guilty, and the opposite of condemnation is justification. God justifies us through our 'faith in Jesus Christ' (Galatians 2:16). The resurrection sealed this.

It ensures that we too will receive perfect resurrection bodies

> By his power God raised the Lord from the dead, and he will raise us also.
>
> (1 Corinthians 6:14)

The New Testament connects Jesus' resurrection with our final resurrection: '... the one who raised the Lord Jesus from the dead will also raise us with Jesus and present us with you in his presence' (2 Corinthians 4:14). 1 Corinthians 15:12-58 is the most extensive passage about resurrection. Christ is called the 'firstfruits' (v. 20), showing what our resurrected bodies will be like. In God's final harvest he raises us up from the dead. Our bodies will be perfect and incorruptible, raised in glory, and fit for eternal life on a redeemed new earth.

It has significance in our lives now

> Therefore, my beloved brothers, be steadfast, immovable, always abounding in the work of the Lord, knowing that in the Lord your labour is not in vain.
>
> (1 Corinthians 15:58, ESV)

Paul's goal is that we focus on our future heavenly reward. The Spirit of God shines the truth and the triumph of Christ's resurrection into our hearts. Such is the influence and power of Christ's resurrection in our lives. It enables and gives us the grace, strength, courage and power to be immovable, no matter what is thrown against us in these last days. Paul once found his confidence in his Jewish heritage and his personal achievements, but now that has been gloriously overshadowed by the triumph of Christ over the 'last enemy', death (1 Corinthians 15:26). From being a persecutor he now is willing to be persecuted for the unbelievable privilege of sharing in Christ's sufferings and his resurrection.[63]

Some Questions

1. Does '[glorying] in the cross' (Galatians 6:14, RSV) resonate with you, or does that feel extreme? Why?
2. Reflect on the truth that Jesus is alive. In what way does this help you face all that tomorrow may demand of you?
3. When Paul talks of the resurrection power of Christ working in you, how does this encourage you in living the Christian life and in ministering to people's needs?

63. See Romans 6:5;

Chapter Sixteen
Adopted as Sons and Daughters in the Family of God

We are becoming more aware that there are many components to becoming an overcomer. In this chapter we will focus on the incredible privilege of being adopted into the family of God as sons and daughters, and grasp afresh what this means. However, we can't leave it there; this leads us on to the importance of the body of Christ, the Church, and its crucial role in giving us protection, encouragement, strength and courage to be faithful to the end. It is embracing the privilege of being adopted into the family of God that then motivates us to be a member of the Church of which Jesus is the Head. Peter adds further to this, comparing our lives to that of being 'living stones' (1 Peter 2:5). The term 'living stones' is used as a metaphor to illustrate the secure and intimate relationship believers have with Jesus, who is described in the previous verse as 'the living Stone' (1 Peter 2:4). Together, these two verses picture how Christ and his followers are joined by God to himself and to one another. It begins by understanding what it means to be adopted into God's family.

Adoption as sons and daughters

> For you did not receive a spirit that makes you a slave again to fear, but you received the Spirit of sonship. And by him we cry, '*Abba*, Father.' The Spirit himself testifies with our spirit that we are God's children. Now if we are children, then we are heirs – heirs of God and co-heirs with Christ, if indeed we share in his sufferings in order that we may also share in his glory.
>
> (Romans 8:15-17)

It seems that Paul is saying, out of understanding and also from personal experience, that the fear of people, suffering and even death itself are reduced in size and power by this truth, and no longer have any hold over his life. The life to come and our reward in Christ become so wonderful that any pain, suffering and persecution here on earth shrink and become powerless.

No longer a slave, no longer separated, no longer under the condemnation of a holy God, but adopted as a son and daughter into the family of God. What a contrast! Why should this be such a crucial truth to understand in the battle of overcoming? Satan, through accusations and temptations, attacks us where we are most vulnerable. Being accepted and loved for who we are, and not for what we can give or do, is important to all of us. And to know that God's love and acceptance is unconditional gives enormous courage and hope. Let's go back into Roman times for further understanding.

In the centre of many markets there was an elevated table and on it were men, women and children chained as slaves to be sold to the highest bidder. New Testament writers sought to represent Jesus' saving activity in terms that convey deliverance from slavery, paying a ransom. This infers deliverance from captivity by means of a price paid.[64] Christ's death is portrayed as the payment price for the deliverance of those held captive by Satan. (The ransom metaphor must be understood in the light of Jesus' offering of himself in obedience to the Father, however, and not interpreted as a payment to Satan.) As the means of redemption, the death of Jesus provides a deliverance that involves not only forgiveness of sin,[65] but also newness of life. Even though Christ's redemptive work

64. See Matthew 20:28; Mark 10:45; 1 Timothy 2:6; Hebrews 9:15.
65. See Ephesians 1:7; Colossians 1:14

is perfect,[66] the redemption of the believer will not be complete until the return of Christ.[67]

Paul writing to the Galatians 3:26-29 says that 'You are all sons of God through faith in Christ Jesus'. Being one with Christ transcends all ethnic, social and sexual distinctions – 'neither Jew nor Greek, slaves nor free, male nor female, for you are all one in Christ Jesus'.

We now see the significance in Roman times of the meaning of adoption, and the depth of meaning it has for us today. There are four main points.

a) The adopted person lost all rights to his old family, and gained all the rights to his new family as a legitimate member of it. 'Yet to all who received him, to those who believed in his name, he gave the right to become children of God' (John 1:12). When we believe in Jesus as Saviour and Lord, God acts by making us a member of his family. 'You are all sons of God through faith in Christ Jesus' (Galatians 3:26). Faith in Jesus takes us from being children of the devil and his family[68] to being children in God's family: 'For he has rescued us from the dominion of darkness and brought us into the kingdom of the Son he loves' (Colossian 1:13). The kingdom is an inheritance which God will give to his people when Christ comes in glory. In that sense the kingdom is both present (we having being delivered from the kingdom of darkness) and also future (at Jesus' Second Coming).

b) The adopted person became an heir to his father's estate, even if other sons were born after him. Because we are sons in the kingdom, God sends the Spirit of his Son into our hearts, and it is the Holy Spirit that gives us the assurance of our adoption, and that produces that cry, '*Abba*, Father' (Romans 8:15). The Holy Spirit brings comfort to us

66. See Hebrews 9:25-28.
67. See Luke 21:28; Romans 8:23; Ephesians 4:30.
68. See 1 John 3:10.

now, and also empowers us for ministry and for living the Christian life. But he also gives us a great inheritance in heaven because we have become joint heirs with Christ – see Romans 8:17 and Galatians 4:7. As heirs we have the rights to an unbelievable eternal inheritance which is imperishable, undefiled, and unfading, 'kept in heaven for [us]' (1 Peter 1:4), because we are children of the King, members of the royal family, princes and princesses who will reign with Christ over the new heaven and new earth.[69]

c) In law, the old life of the adopted person was completely wiped out. All debts were cancelled. Yes, this is a new person in a new life. 'Therefore, if anyone is in Christ, he is a new creation; the old has gone, the new has come!' (2 Corinthians 5:17). As we read in Isaiah 53:4-5, Christ had 'borne our griefs and carried our sorrows' (RSV). The price he paid to cancel all debts from the old life was becoming a suffering servant and being 'pierced for our transgressions', and 'by his wounds we are healed' and a new life begins. *Jesus paid It all for you and me.*

d) In the eyes of the law the adopted person became legally a genuine member of the new family. Adoption is the outcome of saving faith, and one of the greatest benefits that accompany adoption is the way that God relates to us, and then also in the way we relate to one another as brothers and sisters. Perhaps the greatest privilege is being able to speak to God as a good and loving Father, as Jesus taught in the Lord's prayer, Matthew 6:9. As we are no longer slaves but sons, we relate to God not as a slave to a slave master, but as a child relates to their father. We cry, '*Abba*, Father' (Romans 8:15).

We can now see why both for Paul and for us, adoption is maybe the greatest gift of revelation. 'The Spirit himself testifies with our spirit that we are God's children' (Romans 8:16). When we face challenges that

69. See Revelation 2:26,27; 3:21.

are almost too much to bear, the Holy Spirit speaks this truth into our hearts. When we are tempted to disbelieve this truth, what do we say? Romans 8:31-32 gives us the answer:

> If God is for us, who can be against us? He who did not spare his own Son, but gave him up for us all – how will he not also, along with him, graciously give us all things?

It is the Holy Spirit in you and me that gives us the internal witness that God is now our Father. Paul is saying in Romans 8:15-16 and Ephesians 4:30 that it is the Holy Spirit in you and me that gives us the internal witness that God is now our Father. In Ephesians Paul uses the term 'sealing' of the Spirit. A seal in Paul's day was used to guarantee or indicate ownership. Paul is teaching us that the Holy Spirit himself speaks this truth over our lives. The Spirit's presence is God's guarantee that believers are owned by him and secure in him. This is not just for head knowledge; it is to be a spiritual experience which produces a heart cry of worship – '*Abba*, Father'. This is not a minor and secondary matter coming to us in almost an unnoticeable way. Romans 5:5 tells us what is taking place: the love of God is being 'poured' or flooded into our hearts by the Spirit. It is one of the greatest revelations of the Spirit to our hearts. It was the reason the anchor was inscribed on those first century martyrs' tombs, as we discovered earlier.

Could this truth be at the centre of the explosive ministry and Church growth in Acts?

Acts begins with Jesus teaching on the kingdom of God. It is not a political kingdom, but supremely a spiritual one. The same Holy

Spirit that empowered and equipped him[70] to heal the sick, deliver the demonised, release the oppressed, preach the gospel in power to the poor, and to do signs and wonders was to come upon ordinary men and women.[71] Acts 1:1 gives us the reason: so that we do and teach in the same way that Jesus did. This is in line with Matthew 10:25, 'It is enough for the disciple to be like his teacher' (ESV).

The work of the Holy Spirit is to manifest, to make clear to the eye and the mind, to display, show, exhibit and demonstrate the active presence and power of God in the world, and especially in the Church. The first Church grew in an amazing way. In the early chapters of Acts, Peter preached to explain what the Holy Spirit was doing in the lives of people. In Acts 2 we see the growth from 120 to 3,120 believers. Acts 4:4 records 5,000 men believing, which if you include women and children is considered to be about 15,000. All this in just three months! That is about 130 new converts a day![72] By the time we reach Acts 6 there is the need to reorganise the Church for future growth.

> So the Word of God spread. The number of disciples in Jerusalem increased rapidly, and a large number of priests became obedient to the faith.
>
> (Acts 6:7)

A conservative estimate is that the believers numbered 20-25,000 at this time. We continue to see the numerical growth and geographical advance – in Acts 6:8-9:31 among the Hellenists and Samaritans (Judea and Samaria); and then in Acts 9:32-12:24 Gentiles in Antioch followed;

70. See Luke 3:21-22; 4:1,18-19.
71. See Acts 1:8.
72. See C. Peter Wagner, *The Book of Acts* (Raleigh, NC: Regal Books, 2008), pp. 92-93.

in Acts 12:25-16:5 in Asia Minor; and Acts 16:6-19:20 Europe; and finally Acts 19:21-28:31 Rome itself.

Luke is describing the remarkable growth of Christianity through the Roman Empire, which was accompanied with opposition and suffering. Paul teaches in Galatians and Romans that the truth of being adopted into the family of God, and the honour of being able to call God our Father, would enable them to remain faithful to the calling and mission given to them by God.

Even a superficial glance at the book of Acts shows us that the promise of the Holy Spirit not only brings supernatural life and power, but also problems and persecution. In *Acts 4* Peter and John are brought before the Sanhedrin, who threaten them not to speak about Jesus. In *Acts 5* the apostles were arrested and put in jail. They were set free by an angel, but then they were made to appear before the Sanhedrin again. They were questioned by the high priest, and given strict orders not to teach in Jesus' name. Amazingly, they rejoiced to be counted worthy to suffer for Christ. In *Acts 7* Stephen was martyred, and *Acts 8* begins with the apostles remaining in Jerusalem, but the Church was 'scattered throughout Judea and Samaria' (v. 1). In *Acts 9* we see Saul persecuting the Church, and it finishes with the Jews trying to kill Saul, who is now a man transformed by an encounter with Jesus and filled with the Holy Spirit. In *Acts 12* James the brother of John is killed by the sword, Peter is imprisoned, and then set free by an angel. *Acts 14* begins by saying that the Jews who refused to believe poisoned the minds of the Gentiles against Paul and Barnabas, and plotted to stone them. In verse 19 we read that Paul was dragged outside the city and stoned and left for dead. In *Acts 16* Paul and Silas found themselves stripped, beaten, 'severely flogged' (v. 23), and thrown into an inner cell in prison. In *Acts 17* 'Jason and some of the brothers' (v. 6) were dragged before city officials and later released on bail. In *Acts 18* the Jews in Corinth abused Paul. *Acts*

19 sees the silversmith Demetrius stir up the people of Ephesus, who 'seized Gaius and Aristarchus, Paul's travelling companions' (v. 29). *Acts 20* shows that the Jews were continuing to plot against Paul, who in *Acts 21* travelled to Jerusalem, where the Jews once again stirred up a violent crowd against him. He was arrested and bound in chains. In *Acts 22* Paul shares his testimony. In the final chapters, Acts 23-28 Paul faced the Sanhedrin and, being alerted of a plot to kill Paul, he was transferred under guard to Caesarea and to the governors Felix, Festus and finally King Agrippa and Bernice, his sister, before appealing to Caesar as a Roman citizen and finishing up in Rome.

What an anchor being adopted into the family of God is! It brings assurance, confidence and unshakeable hope that nothing can separate us from the love of God in Christ.[73] However, inseparable to this truth is our adoption into the family of God here on earth, the Church.

Members of one another in the family of God, the Church

Acts 2:42-47 places a crucial foundation stone in front of us that we can't ignore. It is integral to our growing, maturing and calling to complete the mission Jesus gave us in Acts 1:8. We rejoice in our fellowship with the Father and the Son through the Holy Spirit. But our ability to be faithful to the heavenly vision and to endure all opposition and overcome is not an individual quality as much as the result of corporate life together in the body of Christ. We hinder our spiritual growth more than any other way by continually asserting our individuality.

There are nearly sixty 'one another' statements in the New Testament. Here are a few – 'Be devoted to one another' (Romans 12:10), 'Live in harmony with one another' (Romans 12:16), 'love one another' (Romans 13:8), 'serve one another in love' (Galatians 5:13), 'Carry one another's

73. See Romans 8:35.

burdens' (Galatians 6:2), 'Be kind and compassionate to one another, forgiving each other' (Ephesians 4:32), '... encourage each other' (1 Thessalonians 4:18), 'spur one another on towards love and good deeds' (Hebrews 10:24), 'pray for each other' (James 5:16).

Earlier we dealt with fear, and Scripture constantly challenges us to not be afraid. That well-known and loved programme *Desert Island Discs* has fascinated and entranced many over the years, trying to imagine just how to personally survive loneliness and isolation. Loneliness involves a deep sense of isolation and disconnection from others, not just on a desert island, but when you feel that you have no one with whom to share the joys and hardships of life. Loneliness is surely something we have each experienced. In times like this we can feel extreme sadness and as this deepens, it can become more like an imprisonment, leaving us despondent towards life. Many have walked through this during tough and unexpected times.

Loneliness is hard to heal. It requires more than just casual social contact – we need to form genuine connections with others on a personal one-to-one basis; hence Paul's emphasis on 'one another', and our belonging to the body of Christ. The writer to the Hebrews also encourages us to 'not give up meeting together' (Hebrews 10:25). The occasions when we have experienced loneliness just reinforce the value and need of a friend and family, whether natural or the family of God. If this is true at an everyday level, it is certainly true in the spiritual equivalent.

Almost everyone has felt lonely at some time. It can be a sign that important needs are not being met, or that foundational truths are being challenged or sidelined. Changing the situation may involve finding and developing a circle of friends, but also securing foundational truths. In times of failure, conflict and persecution, the 'roaring lion' of 1 Peter 5:8) aims to isolate us like a deer or antelope and get ready for the kill.

It is at this point as an adopted son or daughter in the family of God that we see the need to belong to the body of Christ, the Church. It becomes crucial in order to combat isolation and loneliness, and receive the strength and courage to overcome.

There may be the temptation to think that the first-century Christians had some sort of benefit that we just don't have today, enabling them to be overcomers. God has not short-changed us with lesser help than what he gave to his Son Jesus or the early Church. When Jesus said that it was to our advantage that he went away in John 16:7, and returned to the Father, it was so that the Holy Spirit could come and dwell in us. This amazing gift does not mean that the future is inevitable. Branches need to 'abide in the vine' (John 15:4, KJV). Believers need to make every effort and persevere to the end. But what it does mean is that the same Spirit that lived in Jesus, and 'raised Christ from the dead', now lives in us (Romans 8:11). Jesus has given us the same life-giving breath of Almighty God, the Comforter and Counsellor, to lead, guide and keep us faithful to the truth.

We can stand firm because 'He anointed us, set his seal of ownership on us, and put his Spirit in our hearts' (2 Corinthians 1:22).

> His divine power has given us everything we need for life and godliness through our knowledge of him who called us by his own glory and goodness. Through these he has given us his very great and precious promises, so that through them you may participate in the divine nature and escape the corruption in the world caused by evil desires.
>
> (2 Peter 1:3-4)

> We know that we live in him and he in us, because he has given us of his Spirit.
>
> (1 John 4:13)

The apostle John experienced forced isolation and loneliness on the island of Patmos. He embraced this challenge, not with a sense of self-pity but with incredible joy and expectation. The revelation of truth and the presence of Jesus made him aware of the privilege of being an overcomer through faith in Jesus. And as a son adopted into God's family, he heard these words: 'Do not be afraid. I am the First and the Last. I am the Living One; I was dead, and behold I am alive for ever and ever! And I hold the keys of death and Hades' (Revelation 1:17,18). This is a fitting window into the remaining chapters.

Some Questions

1. 'Adopted into God's family' – is that for you more a knowledge-based truth than an experiential one?
2. Is fellowship with others in church a priority for you? What would you miss if you neglected meeting with others, and what do you gain from being part of God's family?
3. Explore the complete list of 'one another's in the New Testament; choose at least three that you believe the Holy Spirit wants you to use in the lives of others.

Chapter Seventeen
Persecution, Suffering and Death Are Not the End

Understanding why the best is yet to come is crucial in giving us the strength and courage to endure to the end. Jesus' main focus and ministry was the kingdom of God. In the Gospels he taught the parables, showing what the kingdom of God is like. It is the reign and the rule of God over every principality and power; it means the defeat of all his enemies. Jesus not only taught about the kingdom; he demonstrated the life and power of the kingdom by the Holy Spirit to heal the sick, raise the dead and cast out demons.[74] Jesus won the battle over Satan first,[75] then liberated his victims through the cross and the resurrection. People saw the kingdom with their own eyes, and experienced personally the life of the kingdom, because the King had come!

God's mission is to re-establish his kingdom. In Matthew 16:18 Jesus tells us how this will be done, by building his Church. The Church is not the kingdom; it displays kingdom life and power to the glory of God. We have already seen this so clearly in the book of Acts. God's programme for winding up history is for the Church to preach the Good News throughout the world. Other organisations and institutions may play an important part in our world, but it is the gospel that enables people to get right with God. This is the Church's primary responsibility.

The Bible story is that you and I can have new life *now*, for the kingdom is *present*. Jesus announced, 'The kingdom of God is near. Repent and believe the good news!' (Mark 1:15), and this involves a new life and lifestyle. But it is also *future*. The kingdom now was made possible through the death and resurrection of Jesus, and the

74. See Luke 4:18.
75. See for example Matthew 4:1-11.

kingdom future will be consummated when he returns in glory. At the Second Coming Jesus will appear in power and glory. God divides his redemptive purposes into two ages:[76] this Age and the Age to Come.[77] This Age had its beginning in creation, but the Age to Come will be eternal.[78] This Age is evil, wicked and rebellious;[79] the Age to Come is the eternal kingdom of God. They are separated by the Second Coming of Christ, the resurrection of the dead, and the final defeat of Satan, sin and death. Life in the kingdom will be realised in its fullness when Christ comes and our very bodies are redeemed. The amazing truth is that this life has entered into our lives now through the new birth, and in that sense *tomorrow is here today*! The future has begun!

We have tasted of the blessings of the Age to Come. The psalmist got it right: 'Taste and see that the Lord is good' (Psalm 34:8). The writer to the Hebrews tells us the future promise of the kingdom is a present reality, referring to those 'who *have* tasted the goodness of the word of God and the powers of the coming age' (Hebrews 6:5, my emphasis).

We can today know and experience inner transformation by the Spirit. The Age to Come has overlapped with this Age, as we read in 1 Corinthians 15:22-26.

The kingdom is supremely 'righteousness, peace and joy in the Holy Spirit' (Romans 14:17). Colossians 1:13 tells us that we have now been transferred from the kingdom of darkness into the kingdom of his Son Jesus. But in the Age to come, God's future and eternal home will be established forever in a new earth and heaven, a perfect environment for our new bodies.

---

76. I have been greatly influenced by George Eldon Ladd's writings here. See George Eldon Ladd, Chapter 2, 'The Kingdom is Tomorrow', *The Gospel of the Kingdom* (Eastford, CT: Martino Fine Books, 2011).
77. See Ephesians 1:21.
78. See Mark 10:30.
79. See Galatians 1:4.

The question I ask myself is, 'Why has this breathtaking future not dominated and impacted the way I live now to the extent that it should have done?' Much of my effort and involvement in ministry has been in seeing the gospel change people's lives. Entry into the kingdom is absolutely vital, but I think I have given minimal consideration, concern and guidance to being a role model in how to finish the race. Perhaps this has been your experience as well as mine. We need together to look at the apostolic focus of Paul at this point.

A selection from Paul's writings that may be helpful

1. He lived and died protecting the wonder of his name being written in the book of life

For Paul in particular, this was not the icing on the cake; it was the cake! Eternal life was for Paul the climax and not an appendix. His fight was against an enemy who desired the individual and the body of Christ to become complacent and careless and shipwreck their faith.

Hebrews brings a very severe warning and, although written to Jewish believers against a backdrop of persecution, it is a practical challenge to all. We have mentioned the importance of the anchor in securing our faith. Now there is another shipping analogy: drifting away…[80] bringing in that sense of lowering the sails, putting us at the mercy of the wind and the waves – and the danger of being shipwrecked on the rocks. The Jewish believers were tempted to drift back to the synagogue and by doing so avoid persecution from Rome. We too may be tempted, when persecution or hardships arise, to return to our old life and lifestyle. Perhaps it is worth asking ourselves three questions. What would cause me to drift away from God? What would cause me to doubt the work of

80. See Hebrews 2:1.

grace in my life? What would cause me to deny all that God has done in my life and has in the future for me?

> Some have rejected [holding on to the faith and fighting the good fight] and so have shipwrecked their faith.
>
> (1 Timothy 1:19)

In verse 20 we read that Hymenaeus and Alexander had rejected and abandoned their faith, making it nothing. Paul was not just exhorting Timothy as if the danger was just for him; it is for us and the whole Church. The former lifestyle of the Corinthians Paul lists in 1 Corinthians 6:9-10, instructs them and us today, to be careful not to slip back into old ways and forfeit a place in the future kingdom. In Philippians 3:7-11 Paul teaches us not to be complacent with regard to the resurrection. His appeal is to live up to what we have already attained, and that means finally standing firm in the Lord. The real danger is being deprived of 'the prize' (Philippians 3:14). Why is Paul such an example? Because he did not just teach the truth and the full will of God – that is, God's eternal purpose by grace to bring salvation and new life to all – but he lived it out.

> I have fought the good fight, I have finished the race, I have kept the faith. Now there is in store for me the crown of righteousness, which the Lord, the righteous Judge, will award to me on that day – and not only to me, but also to all who have longed for his appearing.
>
> (2 Timothy 4:7,8)

The very fact that in Revelation 3:5 Jesus speaks about the possibility of names been blotted out from the book of life is surely enough for all of us to stop in our tracks and catch our breath. None of us can be so smug as to say, 'That applies to others and not me.' At the same time, we need to be aware of feeling hopeless. Under pressure, our inheritance in Christ may seem so easy to lose and so hard to keep, and we end up saying, 'I'll never make it!'

Does this cause us to fear? Most likely yes. But fear is not necessarily negative; it can be a healthy response. Fear that paralyses our Christian lives is obviously not good, but fear that causes us to respond to God is healthy. The Greek word for fear, *phobos*, has more than one meaning. It can mean running away, fleeing panic-stricken from a battle, and the phrase 'do not be afraid' encourages us to stand our ground and fight. Conversely, it is also a feeling of awe and respect, as in Matthew 14:26-33, Luke 5:26 and Acts 9:31. When Jesus walked on water the disciples' fear turned into worship. When people witnessed Jesus healing the paralysed man they were amazed and gave praise to God. Living in the fear of the Lord became a lifestyle as the Church in Judea, Galilee and Samaria were strengthened and encouraged by the Holy Spirit. But the meaning goes a bit deeper than this. It is more than respect; it is a fear of failing to enter into what God has promised.[81] It is a fear of what God can and will do. Can you imagine the look on the twelve disciples' faces when Jesus said to them in Matthew 10:28, 'Do not be afraid of those who kill the body but cannot kill the soul. Rather, be afraid of the One who can destroy both soul and body in hell.' Is this a negative statement? No, it is truth spoken in love by Jesus to his disciples, trusting that a healthy understanding of what it means to 'fear the Lord' will be grasped. When thus understood, it makes us realise that when under

81. See Hebrews 4:1.

pressure or suffering persecution, the fear of what people can do is not worth comparing with what God can and will do. This healthy fear will remove complacency, pride and carelessness, and rekindle a desire to go on believing, go on trusting, go on serving, so that in that position of dependence on God, he may complete all that he has begun to do in our lives. Proverbs 1:7 sums it up: 'The fear of the LORD is the beginning of knowledge.'

'How do I react to this?' We know how impossible it is in our own strength. Our spiritual journey from beginning to end is summed up beautifully in 1 Peter 1:4: 'kept by the power of God through faith' (KJV). But this happens as we believe and keep on believing; as we 'live by faith in the Son of God' (Galatians 2:20), as our overcoming faith is expressed in love and obedient action, and finally, as we stand firm in the battle, and put on the armour of God.

The battle of the mind requires self-discipline. Paul says, 'I beat my body' (1 Corinthians 9:27). Keep moving on with God and being involved in prayer, study of the Word, worship, fellowship, communion and sharing your faith. Live out the apostles' teaching,[82] never forgetting to confess, repent, forgive and walk humbly with God.

2. Paul knew what would happen when he died

Paul's confident and buoyant faith shines through in so many places in the New Testament.

> We are confident, I say, and would prefer to be away from the body and at home with the Lord.
>
> (2 Corinthians 5:8)

82. See Hebrews 10:19-39.

However, it is not just a Pauline perspective. In Hebrews 12:22-23 the writer mentions that when we worship we also come into the presence of 'spirits of just men made perfect' – those waiting for their new bodies at the return of Christ. Finally, in Revelation 6:9-11 and 7:9-10 the souls or spirits of those who have died and have gone to heaven cry out with a loud voice, 'How long, Sovereign Lord, holy and true, until you judge ...' They are there before the throne, crying out, 'Salvation belongs to our God'.

The reason Satan would target the mind of believers in tough times and persecution becomes clear. It is to muddle, bring confusion and dispute about what happens when we die. When this happens, fear and uncertainty return, and our eyes gradually cease to be fixed on Jesus. We become entangled. Doubts and indecision creep into our lives, and trip us up in the race. Perseverance is interrupted, and we begin to drift with an ever-increasing backward look. This is the warning of Hebrews 12:1-2.

This future hope inspires and motivates us. The Spirit imparts confidence in the truth, producing the willingness to endure all things, to the confusion and disbelief of the unbelieving world. Live in the light of what is to come!

Scripture seems to use soul and spirit interchangeably. This can be seen in Luke 1:46-47, 'Mary said: "My soul glorifies the Lord and my spirit rejoices in God my Saviour"'. In John 12:27 Jesus said, 'Now my soul is troubled' (RSV), and John 13:21 tells us that he was 'troubled in spirit'. In Acts 7:59 Stephen cried out, 'Lord Jesus, receive my spirit.' He knew that at death the physical body remains on earth and is buried, but the soul or spirit goes immediately into the presence of God. Paul shared the same confidence; at death his soul or spirit would return to God. What is Paul's reasoning?

In 1 Corinthians 2:14 to 3:4 Paul distinguishes a person who is natural (*psychikos* – soulish) from one who is spiritual (*pneumatikon* – spiritual). The natural person may be defined as an individual who operates entirely on human wisdom. They have not experienced new birth and have no desire to think about God, let alone worship him; their thinking, feelings and decision-making are their own. By contrast, a person born again, made a new person by the grace of God, has come alive spiritually. In Romans 8:10 Paul says that in Christ your spirit (the whole of a person's immaterial existence) is made alive because it comes under the influence and power of the Holy Spirit.

Paul does not fear death. His desire is to 'depart and be with Christ' for that is better (Philippians 1:23) He would rather be 'away from the body and at home with the Lord' (2 Corinthians 5:8), including the confidence that when he dies physically, his spirit would go into the Lord's presence and there enjoy fellowship with the Lord at once. Yes, immediately be in the presence of Jesus. No wonder he could say, 'Death has been swallowed up in victory' (1 Corinthians 15:54). Understanding that the best is yet to come is crucial in giving us the strength and courage to endure to the end.

3. He knew what would happen at Jesus' Second Coming – his new body and resurrection

Paul understood that death is the result and final outcome of living in a fallen world. For believers, death is not a punishment, as there is now 'no condemnation for those who are in Christ Jesus' (Romans 8:1). What is sown perishable is 'raised imperishable'; it is 'raised in glory' (1 Corinthians 15:42-44,49). It is sown a physical or 'natural body', that is, subject to the character and desires of this age. But it is 'raised a spiritual body', that is, consistent with the character and activity of the Holy Spirit.

Imperishable bodies simply mean that they will not wear out, grow old, or be subject to sickness, disease, injury or death – they will be perfect!

Let's follow the sequence of events briefly and reflect personally on them.

1. There is life on earth, when we have an opportunity to believe in the salvation that only Jesus Christ can give. Hebrews 9:27 asserts that there is no second chance after death.
2. At death there is a separation of body and spirit. The body is buried (to be resurrected later), and our spirits go immediately into the presence of Jesus. Jesus said to the thief on the cross, 'today you will be with me in paradise' (Luke 23:43).
3. When Jesus returns in power and glory, our spirit will be re-joined to our new bodies. We will be judged not as unbelievers but by our words and deeds for the receiving of rewards, as we see in 2 Corinthians 5:10.
4. After the final judgement, believers will enter into the full enjoyment of life in the presence of God forever. 'No longer will there be any curse. The throne of God and of the Lamb will be in the city, and his servants will serve him' (Revelation 22:3). The promise of Isaiah 65:17 will be complete: 'Behold, I will create new heavens and a new earth. The former things will not be remembered'.

As we finish this chapter I recall the teaching of Rev Jim Graham about heaven when he pastored Gold Hill Baptist Church, and whose ministry had a huge impact throughout my life.

> In heaven there will be love without passion, for we shall be like Jesus Christ. There will be service without weariness, because His servants shall serve Him forever. There will be holiness without

> imperfection, because His Name will be on their foreheads. There will be blessing without curse, because there will be no more curse. There will be life without death, for there will be no more death. There will be joy without sorrow, for God will wipe away all tears from our eyes. There will be light without darkness, for there will be no night. There will be glory without suffering, because there will be no pain. There will be satisfaction without want, because hunger and thirst will be no more. There will be beauty without infirmity, because we will be without spot or wrinkle. There will be presence without absence, for we will be forever with the Lord.[83]

No wonder our Bible finishes off in Revelation 22:20 by saying, 'Amen. Come, Lord Jesus.' But until that happens, 'The grace of the Lord Jesus be with God's people. Amen' (Revelation 22:21).

83. Jim Graham, *Dying to Live* (NY: HarperCollins, 1984), pp. 137-138.

Chapter Eighteen
Final Words

As I reflect on all the previous chapters, my desire is not that we go away simply with our intellect or understanding quickened in some way. But it is that the Holy Spirit comes afresh upon us, so that we live out and demonstrate the truth of what it means to belong to the kingdom of God. Overcoming life in Jesus needs to be seen as well as heard.

Our heroes have been those who have not only had good theology and understanding of the Word, but who have loved Jesus more than silver, gold, fame, fortune, life and even death. Reading Hebrews 11:35-38 brings tears to my eyes, and to the nominal Christian it makes no sense: tortured and yet refusing to be released; they willingly 'faced jeers and flogging'; they were 'chained and put in prison'; 'stoned … sawn in two', and 'put to death by the sword … destitute, persecuted and ill-treated'.

How can you explain this? It is idiotic and utter stupidity, *unless Jesus* is who he said he is. Jesus accomplished what he said he accomplished – purchasing our salvation, conquering death, defeating every principality, power and evil, seated now on the throne in glory. And that Jesus will return as he said he would return. If this is so, then we are to be so thankful for the life of those heroes in Hebrews 11 – for their inspiration, courage, faith and encouragement that we will be obedient too as the journey we have been asked to travel on unfolds.

Wang Ming-Dao

As a young missionary in Asia I would have loved to sit down and talk with perhaps one of the greatest Chinese heroes of faith, Wang Ming-

Dao. He went to glory in 1991. Every time my wife and I travelled into China I would think of him. He was born in 1900 in poverty in Beijing at a time both of revival and extreme persecution. The Boxer rebellion martyred thousands of Christians, including women and children. I would have loved to have asked him these questions which at the same time give you an insight into his life and faith in Jesus in a particularly tough time for Christians in China.

How did you come to personal faith at fourteen years of age? What really impacted you?

How did God speak to you?

What struggles did you have to believe?

How did you deal with your family, who treated your faith as mental illness?

As you became a pastor, what were your early challenges?

How did God open up an itinerant ministry throughout China?

What were the high and low points? What crucial lessons did the Spirit teach you?

When the communists took control, how did you feel?

When arrested in 1955 and imprisoned, how did you survive twenty-five years of torture and imprisonment?

You had some serious times of doubting in those twenty-five years; how did you come through?

On release from prison, what gave you the strength and courage to preach the gospel and prepare national leaders in China for the coming revival and massive Church growth?

What words of advice and challenge would you give today?

Obviously I cannot answer this final question, but I have a suspicion that his words would embrace the truth of Hebrews 12:1-2:

> Therefore, since we are surrounded by such a great cloud of witnesses, let us throw off everything that hinders and the sin that so easily entangles, and let us run with perseverance the race marked out for us. Let us fix our eyes on Jesus, the author and perfecter of our faith, who for the joy set before him endured the cross, scorning its shame, and sat down at the right hand of the throne of God.

As I reflected on this, it is almost as though I heard the cloud of witnesses giving this advice:

1. Get ready for the final part of the race.
2. Identify and then discard things that could trip you up.
3. The final laps of the race are marked out. You are not running in the dark. The Holy Spirit is shining his light on the glory of the finish line.
4. The Holy Spirit's ministry will enable you to focus your eyes on Jesus and on him alone. He will impart joy, no matter what suffering, hardships and difficulties you encounter.
5. The promise is so amazing, dazzling, inspiring; never let it go!

It is appropriate to finish with two verses of Scripture, one from the Old and the New Testament

> … the Lord is with me like a mighty warrior; so my persecutors will stumble and not prevail.
>
> (Jeremiah 20:11)

> To him who overcomes, I will give the right to sit with me on my throne, just as I overcame and sat down with my Father on his throne.
>
> (Revelation 3:21)

The grace of the Lord be with us all.